The Filatory: Compendium I

THE FILATORY: COMPENDIUM I

gnOme

CONTENTS

Strands

Production (Dis-ease)

Writing finds this space uninhabitable.
Here one senses only two things:
the cold, metallic machination
of multiple threads being forced out of a totality
and strands scavenged from the void.
Abandonment of a singular fabric of reality
in favor of threads spun from somewhere.
This is a machine of pure production
functioning with the sole purpose of creating something
where there is now a deficiency.
Design is apparent in this machine
but the specific purposes of it remain elusive and esoteric.
One experiences a sort of dread
or dis-ease in this device's company.

Threat (Heat)

Guided by the threat of persecution
this seeks to reconnect the dismembered pieces
of ancient and future bodies.
Our time is always a different time
Our place is always a different place
nevertheless
our presence will be felt.
Bonded by our fragmentation
this congregation will not supplicate to dying suns.
Instead, we will generate our own heat.
A heat fueled by generations of the unwelcome cinders
that were used up
left to die out of a strange kind of blindness.
The heat of our presence is imminent and unwavering;
it permeates and threatens substance
precedes the origin
and amplifies of its own accord.
Heat is never contained;
the boundaries and barriers also serve as conductors
for new passageways.
Its properties are simple, but out of these simple principles
inventive catalysts rear infinite complexities.
Do not confuse this heat with
passion, lust, anger, or aggression.
These are invented to entertain and mesmerize.

Our heat is the effect of our own disappearance.
In the end, there is no us, there never was an us
there never was a you
there is only the heat that was left behind
that was always there.

Waste (The Unwanted)

You are in the middle of a swarm.
Language turned movement, pure sound, or into absence
(any of these can be put forward as the point of creation
or cause of destruction).
Better here to speak
with the dumb weight of nothing
than to crystallize those odious mutterings
into something blown away in an arenose wind
like an obsolete photograph.
Fluidity that has no use except to be fluid
to run across, to leak, to drip
a contaminated river carrying
the byproducts and excrement of a species long-forgotten
(food for the animal that still hungers).
If you can stomach this junk debris, then you should feast.
Take a glance—what food is left?
Absence that exhausts with its mass
sound that thieves from the noise around you
movement that lies perfectly still—
again, the interpretation here is all and none.
One thought mirrors another,
a bone in one eye, a bird in the other.
A bone and a bird woven into a garment,
for you are cold
and that coldness will never leave you.
You came because of the cold,
and the broken promise
of a naked glow
emanating from a machine that does not know you
will not react to you—
the glow haunts you, but now you are not here.
And for each thread another interpretation
for why you are not here
haunting a machine.

Rooms (Impermanence)

This is composed of rooms. The rooms are open.
There are no locks, keys, secret passages or trap doors.
Each room is an incision from which reality slowly collapses.
The corners break out to find their angles
finding the degrees in which the dying lie
creating pathways from hidden chasms, exposing the ignored.
They expand through space bound by the threads they create
threads of disintegration.
They intertwine, grasping each other
always capable of strangulation.
There are no bodies here, only weapons.
They live in the belly of silence, forming an echo
a precursor to nothingness and the forgotten.
A warning of impermanence.

Drones (Fluctuation)

To have entered into a space
a small quarantine where the sound is multiplied
a reverberation through endless hallways
containing many cells
with many stairways leading to many floors.
Enclosed here is the voice now different in tone, pitch, volume, and
frequency depending on where one finds itself—
or begins.
At times, all that can be heard is this:
a fragmented whisper breaking off in the distance...
a loud force, a pounding cry
the shaking of foundations, tremblings at the thought that this voice
is near and perhaps comes closer.
This voice is torn and versatile.
This voice is many, projected from a common thread
a continuous thought process
continually dispersing itself.

Luxury (The Unaffordable)

At the terminus of a greatly tired self-indulgence
is the realization that there can be no completion
or abandonment
of the habits it has taught.

Its end lingers in an afterlife of repetitions
requiring no devotion and yielding no joy or fervor.
Still, it has succeeded in providing for itself
bodies
that never fall out of its motion
thriving within the places it has made
arid, desolate, and mundane.
Dehydrating winds reduce all events, thoughts, and things
to the tyranny of small lifelessness.
Necessity is diminished to the point
where every occurrence unfolds
with an air of cold superfluousness.
In persisting within these depleted fields
one chooses to encounter a luxury that concedes nothing.
A luxury whose experience of you does not end with you.
Unaffordable, it is taken without regards
to time, means, or hope.
And it does not offer a moment of placation.
Its succulence lies in caressing the body in order to
separate bones at their joints
stretching each limb into a pretentious reach
where there can be no approaching one's own hand.
What can be grasped are the Useless Devices
the Tapestries...
the Tendrils
that wrap themselves around a demise that compels seizure
not only of selves or each other
but of strangers and shades.

Cloth (The Veiled)

This contains a hooded arch
one that envelops and covers
hides the unrecognized
the ones who seek solitude
who do not want to be found
(though they are always looked for).
This garment is worn by the guilty alone
by those who have done something
and thus blacken themselves in protection.
One is inescapably bound to the imperfection it guards
to its creases and its stains, its rags and its fading.
This is neither the heavy cloak of the executioner
nor the blindfold of the victim

but rather the accessory of a light invisibility
the façade of perception
where one falls into halves
becomes the emblem
becomes the duplicity
beneath the cloth of infinite separation.

Book I.

Secrecy

I.
Preface
(The Terms)

·To reveal not the object of the secret, but to reveal   (Smoke)
the secret of the secret...so as to strike beyond the
boundary of immediate perception.

·To attempt to unveil the secret only strengthens the
circularity which surrounds it, though without an
interruption.

·At the moment of metamorphosis there is nothing
left for it but death. In so far as a secret survives, it
only moves, transfers, expands, reduces, or shifts.
The single possibility of transformation is in
revelation, and revelation indicates the end of all
things—even for the secret.

·Revelation, as an end, is not a finality. The death of
a secret opens space for more secrets, counter-
secrets: territorial, vagrant, three-headed,
cannibalistic secrets.

·They act upon intensity, amplifiers of their own
accord; to point at one in the face is to increase its
intensity.

(Leaves)   ·To move upon it is to breathe down a sense of
urgency, willing its survival, like a cockroach
under the shadow of a foot.

·Legitimacy? Only narcissism and self-interest
could presume to legitimize that which gains
more in illicitness.

·Only envy and resentment will attempt to vilify
that with which it makes deals in the night.

·But even to grant unwarranted credibility and   (Clouds)
due respect toward the secret is not enough.
When to recognize an ally or when to recognize
an enemy: therein lays the secret's demand. It

26

wants the closure of intimacy that it in turn
grants.

·It acts as a shield, an enclosure from which to
hide, while collecting, while storing, energy.

·It acts as a weapon. So long as the secret carries a
will of its own, so long as the secret can dictate
and determine contours of desire, it can arrange
itself accordingly to manipulate those who
pledge their existence to the world.

·Is it enough to say that exposing the secret's secret
leads to the fatality that it is constantly seeking?
Revealing this secret cannot be based on
negation.

·Negation is the foot that tries to stomp the
cockroach.

·Allowance and affirmation: nature does not
negate, it does not stop, it does not entrap, if it
conceals it is only because something else is
opening into view.

·Therefore, only affirmation can overcome the
alienation affected by stagnant theory. Secrecy is
a filter and a portal where one end leads to
affirmation. By this portal, an emergence occurs.

(Grates)   ·Left to its own devices, it turns wreckage upon
those closest to it, including, especially, its
creator.

·The force of secrecy lies within its ability to
substantiate and manipulate desires, but its will
must be harnessed, trained, broken, and rebuilt.

·This process does not come easily and is not for all
to attempt; more importantly, some secrets
cannot be tamed. These ones must be let go.
They must only be allowed to determine
themselves.

·Confined to the pressures of incubation (not   (Chains)

27

negation, but a steady buildup of fruition), a
new language emerges: a counter-writing.

·This language moves outside the secret, into
foreign territories, passing in and out of
communality as one of its own.

·Described are new forms born out of secrecy, bred
in captivity, training within swarms, brought out
into the open, transferable and shifting just as
the secret itself.

·These movements are made possible because the
secret makes a deal with other secrets. This
being one of many benefits gained from making
good with a secret.

·In the showdown with existence the secret is an
amulet with reverse effects: not to ward off evil,
but to bring it closer.

(Mist) ·The secret reveals much more than it conceals at
times.

·A certain revelation of no small importance is the
utility of evil.

·The secret then is not evil in itself, but it allows for
the possibility to instrumentalize evil, and no
instrument carries too much weight to be
disregarded.

·Secrecy is then a weapon as well as a defense, (Screens)
but not one to be taken for granted.

·It turns on its own, it turns against itself, it often
demands more than it is willing to give.

(Code) ·To communicate with the secret, to learn its language,
means to live with it, to endure it as a trial; the
reward being mastery.

·The few who have the touch and certain sensitivities,
the few who see the signals, give nothing away
because in mastering the secret they also owe to it

for its devotion; and so, without thought, the effects
of secrecy are inscribed onto the bodies of those few.
These are endangering individuals.

·These few do not take titles, nor do they take
entitlement for granted; secrecy has no respect for
these qualities.

·Learning its language is to collect a vocabulary of
whispers, glances, gestures, signs, and codes. But a
master of secrecy knows more than just
vocabulary...

·To step into any situation...to see, hear, and feel all
secrets passing and moving, shifting and
transferring, consuming and haunting, guiding and
betraying. Nothing escapes.

·This sensory overload carries a weight, but the **(Lenses)**
question of responsibility is not just of what
should or should not be done, but of how far the
power over secrecy can be brought before the
walls crack and the ceiling collapses.

·The burden comes at recognizing that the secrets
of others attenuate themselves to the ones who
learn their language.

·Secrecy arranges space. In a perfect structure,
nothing moves. If movement is allowed, then it is
because there is a secret hard at work.

·The secrets, in spite of their hosts, linger off,
demanding their own, demanding recognition,
demanding intimacy.

·In order, rank and file, adjustments must be
made, tolerances dictated, the herd-gathering of
secrecy to be unleashed.

(Fur) ·Even those whose secrets are so heavily guarded that
they no longer recognize them will be subject to the
forces of other secrets and the structures they bring
down.

·Pay careful attention to the ones who listen with their skin, feel with their ears, and speak with their eyes; these are the dangerous ones, the ones who care nothing of you, only for your secrets and especially the ones that are not recognized as such, because you betray them.

·Secrecy's only kin is betrayal.

·The grand gesture of existence points towards the secret, a taunt, to rise up, to take it down, because it is indebted to the secret, its very own secret.

·Existence never learned to pay its debts. In the end, existence will be betrayed.

II.
Typology
(The Process)

·In a moment, when exigency crosses initiation, a   (Shards)
principle of redaction begins. In this moment,
the kaleidoscopia of sense undergoes a process of
distillation.

·The eye begins to only see one color (red),
prismatic shapes blend, and trance takes hold.
This picture of purity held by the entranced
arrives out of diffraction, and passes through to
leveling distortion.

·The pure, in this sense, becomes possible from a
total and sweeping violence, where the figures
left behind retain only the miniscule fragments
of their former reality.

·There is nothing new here, only a rebranded and
rabid consciousness, one that conflates the
differences between toxicity and vitality.

(Ashes)   ·What holds most interest is how the lines of
exigency and initiation come to meet; in
particular, the convergence of these lines when

directed out of the many concerted glares, from different stances, toward different aspects brimming from a black-box.

·The presence of this box, or the awareness of the box, or even the awareness of the possible presence of a box, carries a singular force capable of generating much without the need to do anything at all.

·To step away from light without a torch, to lie   (Spores)
down bare in a nest of vipers and explore the rhythms of disquiet.

·Secrecy is the invisible hand that enacts the unveiling—the greedy touch from beyond. It strips power bare, allowing its utter emptiness to escape.

·The other shadow—the invisible hand that enacts the veiling. In doing so, it stands-ready the vessels intended to contain the liquidation of power. One hand undoes the other.

·An economic distribution of opacity, a currency of its own, shifting patterns, and sloppy predictions.

·For as much as is invested into the proliferation of a secret, just as much must stand against the threat of liquidation.

·Oppositional forces are constantly formed and at work, but these are only a guiding disconnect for which luminous fixtures pulsate.

Between the forces of the secret and the non-secret, reside (unearthed) the typologies of the partial-secret, the visible secret, and the disclosure.

(The Partial)

(Vents)   ·This typology guards the entrance into the corridors of secrecy, and does so by way of deals and bartering.

·The space of negotiation with this type grants the most room for maneuvering; it allows for the most space to move, and everything is accessible, but always for the value of something else.

·In order to navigate through the shifty-eyed avenues of the clandestine, one must first determine the topography and then bridge the landmarks.

·The choice to enter these corridors is often an arresting thought raised in the aftermath—once one finds oneself already there.

(Conch)

·In this area, there are no friends, only allies. When desire gets lost to the humidity of interest, and overexposure quickly generates heat, every breath must be consecrated to the extreme limit of value-exchange.

·But even allies can quickly become enemies for the right price. Trust is gauged only by what one has to gain at another's cost.

(The Flick)

·Moral principles learn to betray at the command of a switchblade-baton.

·Betrayal can be purchased easily with just a few careless words, a wink, a smile, or a nod.

·This does not mean that moral principles need to be abandoned at the outset; that would be to simply replace one principle over another; instead, it means to subject them to an exchange-value.

·People, things, ideas, values: all must be examined with the expert-eye of an appraiser.

·Currency in the bartering system is about knowing how much something is worth and for whom. That is: even moral principles can be bought, sold, used as leverage in a deal, or traded for something better.

·The partial-secret transforms those of whom it
affects into black-market entrepreneurs.

·In this arena, there is no all-encompassing
economic animal of which everyone is
invested, and no symbolic currency that
universalizes value.

·Yet in spite of the seemingly simple processes
of exchange, there are numerous
complexities that bind and configure any
given situation.

(The Premature)

·One that unsettles from a birth-too-early...   (Scars)

·Blinds angled down to shut in a derelict silhouette,
track-marks along the veins of an exhausted statue,
the entrance into the area of the partial-secret is
born of a mislaid intimation.

·A scent, a whisper, a strange or foreign body mark,
something left behind, not always there, hooks,
harnesses, grabs, and disturbs, agitates.
(Occurrence): zip-cord. (Continuity): a matter of
perception.

·What comes before the intimation...

(A Pact)   ·An impact, footprints on top of an empty grave:
there must be something that precedes it,
something that binds the drop of anticipation
to the gravitational axis of exigency.

·The blank page in the hidden archive—while
absent of form, it becomes aligned to the
physical reference of the slightest revelation,
and begins to enact a formal response.

·Hyper-sensitivity and hyper-acuity are the
responses of the body compensating for the
sudden awareness of this mis-shape.

·The hidden archive, the storage space, where

33

numerous unformed visions await to take
shape, it is the source of all secrets; the secret of
the secret.

·This is not a zone of exclusion. (Duels)

·It persists through the interminable, the receptive
and the accumulative; no discretion—everything
gets taken in as is.

·The archive only stores. Wherever can be—
connections are made, built upon; to serve as
materials for an ancient guild.

·The servile posture never gets distracted, ascetic,
astute (feudal but not of feudalism). Acerbic
without wit, without the blindness of a gesture,
unpliable, and especially unpalatable.

·A force of accumulation: stopping for nothing, it
aims at all: accumulates, and, through this
accumulation, plunders.

·The blind arrangements proliferating out of the
archive's duty to itself (to amass interminably)
leaves ruptures of disconnection.

·A blank page, or an unsigned document—a
decree, or an item of unheralded evidence, these
clerical reserves most likely drown within the
expansive mass of the archive's storage space.

·Other times, however, they resurface, and in
doing so, they find little recourse in a commerce
that has given no context for their existence.

·In this case, the guilds, the brokers and the
dealers, work in silent cooperation in order to
make all the pieces fit together.

(Dust)   ·Too many disconnected items floating—when the
pieces will not fit, the mounting heap of a
junkyard-carnival, then aggravating possibilities
begin to stroke the bells of doubt.
·The process cannot be stopped because the archive

has an insatiable appetite for what it cannot ever
completely digest.

(The Visible)

·That which can be seen, but not spoken of: (Lightening)
a candle-whip that steals the fire from
grey tongues…

·That which learns to hide out in the open:
out of necessity, out of mind, because to
survive is already too much. It begins
unearthed, in crumbling, from a soundless
drift out into the air.

·Breathable in any language: an erosion of
light, sullen, without loss, biding time
amongst disease, the sickening, the
tremors, and the castrated…

·That which is known but never quite
revealed (relived, relieved): the tide's
return to wipe clear the sand…

·That which insinuates the common tides of
torn horizons: of the touch from beyond,
the touch of alien tears, the irreversible
touch…

(Revelation)

The visible is available to everyone, but not everyone knows that it is
a secret…collusion…some know something, while others do not…

(Arrows)   ·Behind the figure in the forest, a figure without
shadow, it mimes towards nothing—there is
nothing there. Feeding from the roots, age-old,
and fossilized, of the trunk left in memorial
standing in the way; the recalcitrant figure
vanishes from the scene, only knows vanishing.

·A voiceover from another world speaks to us
openly of this figure—it is vanishing, and all
the while one hand guides our attention

toward a banquet feast where lively terraces
overflow with the charmed and charming.
There is glass in the air; be careful where you
breathe, but also, be careful where you laugh.

·A slick master who flings from the teeth, no
deeper than the gleam of pure white, takes the
front and speaks with a voice from another
world. The fire-side glow: whispers that flicker
and glimmer, shamelessly teach the stories that
never teach anything, all the while knowing
that there is no need to teach anything at all.

·They all command, wrapped in crystal
packaging-paraphrasing, gifts of gold and lead,
but the alchemy occurs elsewhere/outside.
The other hand sweeps in, points in another
direction, from where a small crowd being
glazed over bends in unison, leaning inward
towards the voice from another world, who
speaks, whispers: there are always more
charmed than charming.

(Relive)

The Emperor's new clothes. Family dinners.
Futility...Faithless movement...

·Identify and grasp, visualize and squeeze,   (Arches)
compression and tension, synecdochic
movements made by an arch (from particular to
general: small to large) in construction block by
block, from the ground up, building to create a
perfectly self-supporting structure: biting,
clamping, the view of beyond, there can be no
horizon so long as buildings stand in the way:
difference between arches, buildings, and
forceps—illusions, transcendental illusion,
pathological consciousness...

·How then to proceed? To speak of what cannot be
spoken of, and yet, giving the taboo a name will
only weave the incision.

(Fascia)   ·Tense and muscular, forceps squeezing the skin,
folding into bunches, pulling apart flaps, lids,
linings; clamping down on the vein, lock-jaw;
tense and fascicular, trained to endure the
ever-tightening, without seizing, splicing,
cutting; measuring with focus so as to become
function while not reducing, not compressing,
and not condensing. There is nothing of the
stolid cobblestone arch found within each of
its own blocks, held together through its
particulars toward the stability of the whole.

·This instrument creates points of definition,
irreducible by implications of necessity,
expansive at the outset, at onset, once the site
is prepared the view turns outward, stretched
along the skin. Bring it back, close in, with a
sterile towel the site is dressed to box out the
surrounding area: a dual-performativity, at
once to maintain the sterility of the localized
environment, but also to zero in against the
ever-expansiveness of the surface area.

·Secrets survive by manipulation and
misdirecting, and so, against the backdrop of
localization, as in the lethal-injection site
swabbed with an antiseptic, there is something
else going on: something visible, all too visible.

·The many scrubs upon scrubs of soap, sterilized
water, betadine, and alcohol, neither stop nor
interrupt secrecy from proliferating or
replicating—in mutation there is muteness;
concealment, effected by sterilized towels,
surgical gloves, masks, and eye
protection...layers upon layers.

·Watch how secrets move in these micro-zones of
confinement. Watch how they spread in the
under-passings of dense superficiality. Bring
down the forceps and the scalpel: to clench
and to lacerate, because it is not enough to
speak of previous, impermanent, and episodic
eviscerations. Watch how secrets move in these
micro-zones of opening.

·The imposition of sterility, a vacuous
environment, is meant to keep the many
secrets of the body contained, non-
transferable.

III.

Weaponry
(The Arsenal)

(Whispers)(Critical Arsenal)

(Switchblades)

(Concealment)

(Tongue) (Ear) (Digestion)

(Death by a Thousand Cuts)

(Whisperer)
(the wink/secret-driver/command/
herd/noise/delirium/flick/threat)

Bringing the secrets into a herd, driving them, whipping them,
enraging the gathering; few things can compare to the threat of a
stampede: the ground trembling with anticipation, dust clouds
emerging, flooding the air, the muffled squeals of the smaller ones
being torn asunder. There are two positions one may find oneself in
amid such a situation: standing before the cloud, awaiting the force
behind the thunder, or, to be amongst the fury, blinded, exerting,
and keeping ahead.

Standing before the stampede means to confront inevitable
claustrophobia—when timing does not permit a way out. When
running and attempting to outrun is as absurd as clenching fists,
especially when there is no one to see the false bravado. What is the
difference between standing before a stampede, sitting as an
audience member in a brass concert, and bearing witness to your
worst nightmares? Confronted by the greatest of all perils, there
meet the demands of risk. These intersecting drives are all subject to

one cause: how to become an active force even in death. Because in death one can be either active or passive, but to be active is not to be legendary or iconic; in fact, these are the most hardened states of passivity.

One cannot assume that to be within the storm-crowd-trembling grants one the drive of being an active force. Exigency calls for movement, blindness, anaesthetized by hypersensitivity, and a misguided rush for survival; these conditions are fuelled by a single principle: always more. To be subject to the herd-swarm means to be caught up in a force, one that exceeds what the eye points out, and one that defies what can be articulated. In order to understand, there is only the willing acceptance of this raging: to be consumed from within. From the rage, the torrent-biting, aligned with a constant search for the end of all things, one achieves the weight of an active force—especially in death. The driving procession begins with two orders to step through: to be consumed from without, posed against the fury, and to be consumed while within, generating the fury.

Neither position is an end-point, nor a badge of honor. This means that the drive that brings one to this position cannot be stronger than the drives that are to follow; simply because, when taking up this course, there is a responsibility to reciprocate in turn. Even at the point of standing within, generating the fury, there is only a minor contribution to what is already there. Holding to this position for too long will only cause one to be trampled, or, as is often the case, one will find oneself again positioned outside and against the herd. But to be pushed and pulled, thrown between and without, being subject to the catalytic catastrophe grants one a refined sensitivity for the ability to orchestrate. An operational manager of force—gathering secrets in order to rise above and command the trampling.

Whispers, the whisperer, the secret-driver: the procession leads forward, once gathered and won over by the trampling, it brings forth the third. But first the trampling: to be trampled upon, to trample over. To be trampled on well enough so as to disregard the trampling that needs to occur. There comes a certain pleasure with the ability to whisper in someone's ear, "I am going to walk on top of you and crush your skull, and I will tell you exactly how it is going to happen..." In order to fulfill this threat two things must occur: the threatened must not believe the threat, and the subsequent unfolding of events must be so well predetermined that it becomes finality. If it were the case that the one were to occur without the other, then the mark would be missed. To fulfill on a threat is not just to complete it, there must be a break in awareness, confronting and rewiring anticipation, breaking expectation. Taking control of a moment of disbelief, this is the actual moment when the skull becomes trampled; everything that follows is a mere eventuality.

The orchestration of gathered secrets always pursues a threat. What points of desire to push on, by what manner of revelation or concealment, by what possibility that should not or cannot occur? This is the configuration of placement that rises above the gathering, it pulls forward to dictate, to determine, and to persuade by force. First and above all, this placement is not a given, it can only be taken. Taking is a challenge when dealing with secrets, because secrecy demands indirect methods; it compels by way of misdirection. The whisperer is the forceful one who learns the language of secrecy, overrules the herd-gathering, and conducts its movements in waves of energy. No longer subject to being consumed from within or without, it levels fields, barren and trampled, but with the intimate knowledge of having been on the other side.

(Quantity) (Quality)

(Spread) (Incubation)

(Shortsighted Accumulation) (Tolerance)

(Ingestion)

(Addiction) (Adjustment) (Actualization) (Toxicology)

...because all things are poison,
the secret too is no exception...
...at what dose does the secret become poisonous?...
...to begin again with the wager...
...the possibility to get more than what is to be expected...
...seduction from the offering of chance...
...a resilience against what has already been written...
...an alibi on its own terms...
...to offer up a small gain of grandiose proportions...
The third gift (Mjöllnir):

...brings silence...
....a hammer borne from arcane fires, an interruption,
and breath, solid breath....
....a good wager, a good secret,
will always grant more than what is offered...

...much more...
...a catalytic convergence...
...drip by drip...
...secreting to (.001) degree...
...works its way into the system...

the other side of the secret exposes the doses
for which all things become poison:
hail to the tonic
administer the right dose, at the right time,
for the right one...
...the toxicology of secrecy deals only at the (.001) degree level...

...the line was already drawn...

...only the poison has been waiting to spill over...

...adjustments will always follow...

(Distribution) (Rhythm) (Repetition)

A bridge toward normalcy, if sustained, will hyper-attenuate everything toward the succession of each drop-point. The remaining degrees of detail fall short in accordance to the timing that is expected to occur. Anticipation and remembrance only move for and against the immediate past, or toward the dose that is soon to come: at this point the (quality) and (quantity) can be adjusted with minor details.

The (.001) degree—no longer concerned with the zero-degree, what has already occurred is part of the toxicity. Nothing should be disregarded. At any event, the focus is on the minimal distribution changes that produce the right effect over time.

(Chemical Wagering)

Synergistic $(1+1=3)$

Entropic $(1+1=1)$

Agonistic $(1+1=2)$

Antagonistic $(1+1=0)$

(Admixture)

Synergistic: the concurrent effect of combined secrets (partial, visible, etc.) that results in a wider berth of intoxication.

Entropic: when the collision of secrets results in a reduction to the expected effects of each individual secret.

Agonistic: each secret brings forth the expected equal results upon synthesis. No greater or reduced effect—only the degree of combined expectation.

Antagonistic: nullification from opposing secrets. The possibility to ingest a poison with immunity through a developed intimacy with its antagonist.

(Little Vials of Open)

Bottomless horizons encapsulated in glass, made for ingestion, mixed explicitly for a single consciousness, because even the Open can only be stepped towards by unwinding a given perspective. A drop of the Eternal Forgotten, mixed with two drops of Unchained Voices, might have a lasting effect for some and not others.

To master the alchemy of the secret means to be intimately acquainted with the toxic intimations, suggestions of nothing, and the lethal narrative-disrupting injections, as well as the many different combinations of the quantities and qualities. (Tolerance) no longer seeks to smooth over the gaps left by the secret; it becomes a force that builds toward a greater keep of ingestion. But even then, there can be no formulaic approach to either diagnosis or administration: there requires a fevered receptivity (Addiction) toward the surface movements of all who easily dismiss what is nevertheless going to occur.

42

To produce a wielding variant of systematized and ordered chaos.

Suspicion

Introduction

This paranoia is loosed, initiating a temporary paralysis, as an imperative: become mobile, and create when confronted with this potentially stunning haze; and to draw first blood, become hostile toward all that is tolerant, consoling, comfortable—in short, arresting. These silent threats cannot be left uncontested. This imperative arises from the nothing, arises out of the confrontation between restlessness and non-meaning, at once radically separated from a world and immersed in it. It testifies only to the fact that these things of which it speaks are somewhere, and not of their reality or truth. At least a mild degree of suspicion is advised, and so it must never be supposed that anything is merely accidental, circumstantial, or insignificant. These tendencies are building toward something which must be concealed:

1) A crime against the mind
2) A crime against some other body that the mind would not permit
or
3) A bodily suicide

One must be suspicious of these idle tendencies of the body, of the fingers and hands that never cease movement, where days wasted on the meaningless—the countless—become indiscernible from the rest. The tasks of perpetuation, and the futile attempts for something worthwhile. All of this is planning, accumulating force. Wasteful times though extremely active...

...where the hands do not simply move involuntarily—or even for the most obvious, practical purposes—but for reasons unknown...

These are phenomena that demand explanation, that cannot be overlooked, that are indicative of something: the practice for some future event, a sort of preparation or honing of skills. These bodies are plotting something of which it is necessary our minds remain ignorant. For what crime is the body plotting, and why must the mind be excluded?

Ungrounding

Time: Questionable

Past: Muted

Time to become convinced that those closest to oneself were positioned to be detrimental. This positioning is one of hostility.

Present: Anechoic (without reference or origin)

Paralytic (groundlessness).

New means of movement/communication/translation/transgression must be crafted. Transformation from a solid existence to one of liquidity, aerialilty, miasma, dust.

There is action, but it is deflated, devoid of its former meaning. It takes on a malleable quality, now shaped by the hammer-blows of inscription. Precision instruments, sometimes for no specific task, forged from dust and air, by force...always by force. This exercise counteracts life: counter-stasis, counter-reality. Everything stands against it, and, where actual enemies are lacking, it crafts those as well. This is a process that requires (desires?) hostile engagement, with itself above all others. It simultaneously finds and creates conflict, taking all comers, in hopes that it may encounter one capable of remolding it, altering its trajectory. An epoch is forgotten. Another approaches in which references to a past fall silent. These attempts simply have no referent, no currency. Things formerly assumed, pre-given, immutable—have vaporized. They take on a certain lightness that dematerializes, no longer allowing them to function, now lacking an assumed right to existence and operational potential. They have become aerial, weightless.

The mere suggestion of an alternative has subtly untethered them, and that it took so little to do so is remarkable. These incomplete articulations of an outside have the capacity to ruin. This is not the monumental upheaval of a world, but the muted, unnoticed ungrounding of something now left to evaporate, drift, dissipate, reconfigure, and reorient. A minor undoing, brought on by a glimpse that offers nothing: no return, no advance, no solace. A cruel glimpse that will not reward cooperation and can only fulfill inherent threats upon failure. It places one at a precipice, trapped between a world—the return into which is impossible—and an infinity. It demands movement from this precarious position: quite an impossibility. And impossibilities are exactly what are exercised here, following only the forgetting.

Future: Background Noise (nervous energy, remnants, discarded knowledge)

Rustling, restlessness, soft intonations of idle movement, amplification of the insignificant. There is a heightened sensitivity, an attuning to the ignored. This modality resembles a return to a primitive state in which one is suspicious of even those motions and noises that cannot be attributed to something significant, a state in which the rustling of a branch in a breeze elicits an alertness. Now, though, there is only rustling. An inversion of significance, though this inversion is one of horizontality. The distant, distorted, unknown becomes central, the focus. To have many decentralized focal points: this apparent impossibility is what indicates inordinate suspicion.

A future of restlessness is forged on a horizon (strange things always occur on horizons).

Space: The Net

Position: Entangled

Constructed of the same familiar materials as the world's constricting discourses, but in a way that is slightly off and will force one to sever *those* ties in order to escape *this* net.

Dragging: Contamination and Dispersal

To bear this burden

To catch, snag, and drag as one passes by

To wear this net as a mark upon one's back, as a scar that at once reminds of a forgotten yet clearly-imagined past, and forebodes of something unforeseen. To redistribute debris in places it does not belong. The introduction of invasive species, immune to the defenses of their new environments, granted greater potential simply by virtue of their exoticism and displacement. To become contagious, touching everything, infecting open wounds, and opening new ones for further infection.

Though this message is not trustworthy, it contains information, which in a state of groundlessness, is one of the few forms of currency that remains.

Conspiring

I.

The hands possess seemingly infinite energy, energy that is most commonly dissipated in idle tasks, executed only to maintain dexterity and skill for the more severe.

II.

The very act of inscription arose only to occupy the hands while the mind expounds all its superfluous concepts, images, and narratives.

This writing is manual, not cognitive: thought belongs to the mind, while this act is solely of the conspiring body. And yet, the physical inscription carries more significance than its origin (the idea).

> Yes, all the millions of pages covered in meaningless writing: that was all done to increase dexterity for another purpose, a purpose yet unknown, in the same way an obsessive craftsman will hone his tools and products to absolute perfection simply to shelve them. These are no wasted artifacts, merely crafted and shelved so as to be allowed to deteriorate, but the instruments of an approaching event.

No, this is not the sort of being one overlooks.

III.

The most dangerous writers are those who agonize so as to perfect every line with full knowledge that these lines mean precisely nothing (in their time), for these are the ones who are contributing to an ever-growing stockpile. A time approaches in which a new breed will find themselves equipped with a vast inventory of instruments.

IV.

World-altering theories arise out of thought and writing

Revolutions in the name of ideas

Populations die off or are cleansed away for various rhetorics

And all of this is done so the conspiring body can continue its reign over the mind, and for no other purpose than this:

Entire populations sacrificed because this body must adapt, improve, prepare, and feed its consumptive desires, not in an attempt to satisfy them, but precisely to perpetuate and even magnify them.

And all so a primordial blood-lust, with a taste for its own, be fulfilled, and for no other purpose than this:

This body's obsolescence has nearly reached its completion, and precisely because it is understood to be superfluous, it is afforded the luxury of planning a more extensive onslaught.

No longer burdened with work necessary to its survival, it is allowed all the leisure it requires to refine its skills and form, for the event toward which it is moving.

V.

All that is supposed to have occurred as a result of mental work (theory, discovery, rhetoric, ideology) is the doing of an unnoticed mastery, one afforded unending liberties and capabilities by its obsolescence.

VI.

At the moment of thought's inception,

this brute mass sensed its looming obsolescence on the horizon,

and not by any faculty, but purely from instinct it crafted a method to ensure its endurance...

...that most prized possession...

...that thing that distinguishes this hideous being from the natural world...

...that thing in whose name terrible acts have been committed...

cognition was turned into backbreaking, manual labor

and thus a species remained enslaved to its physical reality

VII.

Even as writing moves away from the manuscript and toward other technologies of procession, the hands remain essential to this document. The aversion felt toward other forms of recording one's thoughts (visually, aurally) is no accident. This is not merely the result of technological limitations or complications; no such barriers exist. Writing must remain manual, and any shift that removes the hands from this process will mark a significant transition, deviating from the conspiracy that must take place.

VIII.

It is by something like a design that the minds of exception are compelled to record thoughts, a compulsion forced upon that cogitating mass of fat residing in the skull, that entity that is at once mental and physical. To acknowledge the reign of the forearms. These performances are as superfluous as writing, but without the delusion that thoughts must be recorded to manifest in the world. Rather, they are relegated to an incendiary unreality, where thought and words attain unnatural ignition, as photometric instruments, gauging the brilliance of a flash. These words are understood as superfluous. This is no writing, but the forging of components for an accumulating apparatus.

IX.

Autonomy cannot be given to the mind or to the self, in order that it remains docile. A vast array of violences are perpetrated against those who believe themselves to be unbound: arthritic joints, severing of fingers, abandonment of limbs, forgetting of nails, dematerialization of eyes. Those who have extended such autonomy, those who have remained docile, are encountered by an unforeseen conclusion: extinction by the mere glimpse of an alternative, an alternative that leaves one stranded in-between, demanding that all be forsaken for continued movement.

X.

Will the body usurp something from the mind? This question proceeds from crumbling foundations. It is an indifference that has allowed the mind to run wild for millennia, all the while, unwittingly, becoming more and more a *manual* being, a being of hands. Something is shifted away: a substance of labor, where thoughts weigh upon those who carry them, who are taken in by their severity.

XI.

To say that these idle activities of the body are not for anything would fail to decode the phenomena. Think not of what is true, but of what is required to believe and enact any particular proposition. The one who supposes that these tendencies are purely nervous, amounting to nothing, expresses a degree of naiveté and excessive trust in these surroundings. It has been said once before, but this time: a high caliber of suspicion is advised in this place, and so it must never be presumed that anything is accidental or meaningless. These tendencies are building toward something. Any theory with exceptions, anomalies, or questions that it is content to leave unanswered is insufficient.

The Writing of
the Haunt

Weavings of the thread machine:
concepts, sealed (petrified), around which one hovers.

Entanglement/Flaws

Hovering lends to a particular rotation, to a fastening; to drag chains requires a magnetism (objects collected against objects surrounded, a collusion of intelligences; watch for the worlds they conspire against). In this movement one is given over to the terror or ecstasy, perhaps both, of a haunting that demands, calls, that murders, breathes life into, that thieves, rakes across; a violence malformed, hovering-imperfecta (spectral gaze is entanglement, abrasion; whether it be at the object, from the object, or from inexistent forms that seek their own ends out of the failed abortion of their shaping).

Objects/Vantages

Indeed, the object is key. The specter has lost even the false sense of freedom, has abandoned the idea of unfastening (though here, it may have nothing to keep it latched). One becomes bound by one's own voice echoing in a diaphanous fog, a bad air that has commingled with both the birth-cries of the inexistent and the silence of nothing (the specter's wail, in this fog, becoming another object that ensnares). The (erratic) equation(s) of the haunt: whether the specter hovers from object to object, whether what the specter surrounds has become undifferentiable, or whether the proliferation of specters (collection/dispersion)—traces found in each haunt (ghastly scars)—secures a multiplicity of vantage points. Perhaps all and none of these.

Amnesia/Grazing

The given history is a bad one, enclosed in its own impossibility, in labyrinthine libraries, caverns of unknown effects. Tremors felt: interruptions in the false continuum of thought that plague our sensations. To awake in an age of amnesia—stupefied hoverings around the narratives of how we died, why we died—to lose everything yet ask for nothing in return, to grant clemency rather than to interrogate. And, in this sinkhole of bad history, to lose the fascination and astonishment of a spectral grazing that weaves its way in and out of these damning machines and encasings.

Circularity/The Graveyard

If one wishes to continue to slip into the folds of these objects, so be it. Regardless, the writing of the haunt comes from another outside: a time and place that does not exist, cannot exist…as if the image conceived the specters haunting this very page, this very line. An assemblage of (false) impressions that pulses backwards, forwards; an understanding of the circularity, the aforementioned rotation of its existence (a shroud-haunting that envelops this rotation). Within itself, then, this engagement wagers one against another—the ensnarement of the circular versus the wilderness (the outside, or here, the graveyard)—and in this wager it calls upon the gale force of the graveyard's still wind, itself a nonsense, itself the judge of such an encounter, a wager in which the very presence (absence that moves) of the specter hangs in the balance. Implosion: as the specter is erased, everything else with it.

The Unfamiliar/Encryption

One arrives at a space of haunting in search of explanations; the space itself, however, has become wholly unfamiliar. A confederation of lost warnings, one of the forgetful specter: unknown reasons, unknown terrors. Here, as will be encrypted: more a wail (again, muffled, echoed, heard before) than a missive.

Conflation of secrets—another collusion has wormed its way in—the possibility of unfamiliar codes—further, traces that cannot be traced back. Ciphers, vanishing—the writing of the haunt contains the logic of absence, where one is driven into the gaps—the piecing together of frigid limbs, pale thoughts—(the monster of indifference: mirror reflection of the trampled, the terror always coming)—the cipher, at the end of its workings, that generates further hiding-potentials, those lost in the very moment of discovery.

Cryptology has been given to (or stolen by) the machine. The writing of the haunt has become its own anachronous machine; better yet (no, worse), it is the impossibility of this machine's death.

You have found yourself, then, in the crypt of the impossible.

Phantasmagorical Principles

Sickness

(Haunting that percolates)

(Spectral decay: a plague of ingestion engendered by a species that failed to realize its death, failed its last ablution, failed to raze the remnants of moulting.)

A principle of three: an age vanishing, a vanished age, an age of vanishing...

An age's third atumbra: glimmerings of a machine (the third star's occluding body) that operates in the third freezing...

A machine of dialysis...
    A third affliction: vesanic cachexia, the wasting of madness...
      A third contagion: coalescence of word and mold...
      A third rash: ghosting edge of tundra spreads;
         irritation, the third eye twitches...
      A third lancing: pedal edema of the third foot...

With the vanished age, a vanished dawn—a vanished promise—the driving out of these specters has led to further collection and further proliferation. A vanished body (spectral collection, then, residing in the third room)—a purging that has led way to enervation—enervation that has led way to wasting—wasting that has led way to bloat, the bloating of this vanished age's ashen skin (or did you not think it was encased, it could decompose?). One need not imagine the smell, it is in the nostril's third chamber; the smell of grinding teeth, the smell of cracking joints...

      sickness driven out, sickness returning.

Spectral presence to the vanished, before the green dawn: a dose of night terrors. The green dawn arisen, an age of vanishing hovers...

      the third gathering.

The writing of the haunt, mechanism of this age: vertigo of sickness—third wave of nausea—congestion that blankets—writing of bone-keys—third accumulation of the accursed...

58

the third overdose.

Agitation

...all of existence, the graveyard...

...up-pull of chthonic articles...

(objects that haunt)

A broken frame, rusted pendulum, telephone left unhooked: agitation, born of nervous motion, hardened into a point of contact...

A threadless candle, cane sawed through, noose removed from the rafters: agitation, electric, working its way out of the body; a return to take hold, unable to leave or let one escape...

A stranger's trunk of letters, hollow book, poem dated three days from tomorrow: agitation, towards the pitch of frenzy, frenzy that misleads, a smog stirred by compulsory advances...

...coffin choked with objects, where one hangs in limbo, tauten rope; aching delirium, straining to see these specters come and go...

...when they have left for the moment, the writing on the wall hangs as contradiction—and that writing is whiteness, a whiteness that works its way into the words left over, the afterbirth of past engagements—words piled up as bricks—to find that these words were only a kind of paragoge to this whiteness, the faded whiteness of nothing's eye...

...whiteness that reads you...

...whiteness that grows impatient with the answers you have not given, for you cannot answer questions that have not been asked...

...whiteness that decrees the unsettled operation,
this agitation now burrowing in:

The penury of this exsanguine horde
has given rise to the trichotillomania
of thought's copied body,
picked clean as one picks meat off bones.
The stories mapped out in those exposed nerves

are not of the worlds that will be,
but of the ones that are always ending.

Coldness

(If I may, for a moment, relay half-precisions regarding the
exhumation of these bodies. The room grows colder; there are those
who fear that I will freeze before finishing)

———————

Some unnoted town's fringe.
Revenants hang ignited in the gallows for their sordid crimes.
Atmospheric, downwind shifts.
The icing-over has begun.

———————

(And now I freeze)

———————

Exhumation, where the uncovered and unburied meet.
The dead outnumbering the living.
Dehiscence of sutured earth.
Revelation of those who have become overturned.

———————

(My chair is uneven)

———————

Bone-shivers finish their measured coil.
An ice of incompletion.
Taunting the untrained eye.
Cataract of the eye.

———————

(Perhaps they will find me in the morning. I had all intentions of
paying, you know)

———————

The dead are roused.
Iced-over tongues.
Roused to watch the ice form.
The ice forming on your tongue.

————————

(And to think, she said night would fall without disturbance. I have used the wrong words here; I can barely keep from laughing)

Divagation

What is this silence at the heart of silence, if not an excoriation?
What then is this excoriation,
if not the very crest of the unreasonable?
The excess of illumination has induced a backlash of darkening;
now, in that darkness, the heart of silence hastens its once-slow flay.

Haunted language comes at one as fugue and echolalia—strata of spectral murmurings that bend imbibed sounds—speech heard as wails. From which direction does it come, and whom does it repeat? From a mirroring of the host—to a mirroring of itself—to a mirroring of others (the specters before and the ones after).

Repetition cannot entwine in totality; its loose ends become threads that lead astray. Haunting that leads from impossibility's crypt to impossibility's cenacle—a journey in which one becomes cancrine— hovering into passageways not intended for use (nor were they intended for construction)...

yet to forget what was left underground
is a reverse-repetition of these wails, these mirrorings...
yet to forget what was left underground
is a reverse-repetition of these murders, these terrors...
yet to forget what was left underground
is a reverse-repetition of these tremors, these convulsions...

Reverse-repetitions, sounds doubling back on themselves, sounds of silence carving at its heart, for this excoriation arrives in breaking waves of whispers and of rants. The specter wrenches one through the sunken chambers of these whispers, through the searing maelstroms of these rants...

...a haunting no longer to be understood,

but to lead astray, to be misunderstood...

...each wail building the heart of silence already there...
...the heart that flayed you before...
...and readies, on your back, to flay the rest that stand...

Inevitability

Death-drones of the clock's backward hand.

To carry the chains of unnecessary time...

...to construct the cadaver of one's former body...

...to rewrite the works that have burned...

A clock setting one in violation; first read, then felt.
The hand serves as gnomon; its invention casts all in shadow.
Reversibility has a sound: the plodding ticks of this device.
On the horizon, sands of counter-hours approach.

...a specter perambulating the nothing that came before
its haunt rather than the nothing that will come after...

...the further it draws you away from a single end,
the more you begin to resemble its countenance...

death-drones, swarming...

the impression of a hook marks these pages
wresting lacunae towards the center-point
wresting them toward the nothing-before

End-Principle

nothing left but to crawl over you

Textual Murder

The Graveyard (I.)

Writing, the murder

death of an unknown form

for each page, another grave

In this murder, no longer to speak of writing

(disappearance/the vanishing)
(the pale glow of the graveyard, night has moved upon you,
the still wind burns)
(the owl's eye stands as witness)

scratching

(spectral vestiges)
(scratching begs a return)

blood-seizures (phantasmal operations)
spectral gestures (war-performance)
the written has returned unwritten, lost form

haunted ones
alone, in the graveyard
death of Death

(Death becoming Concept)
(Concept becoming Absence)
(Absence becoming Haunting)

Elusion. The owl's eye gives no account.

Immediacy. The owl's eye gives no lapse.

scratching: the release
the written has returned, unwritten, spectral
you as host
war-performance: a summoning

To scratch is to draw blood and to bleed. The movement, the

gesture, is mirrored by counteraction. One is stripped bare, clothes torn, hands maligned, ears punctured

one cannot talk, cannot taste

so blind that even darkness leaves you

(spectral discharges)

(skin-mist, the graveyard's cloak)

congealment—blood/mist—impurity/waste
a river runs through
a scratch that breaks open the dam

The written has returned, unwritten

they remain stained by the vestiges

the dam is broken, flood impends

The graveyard—catastrophe rests its head. Violence becoming playful, delicate, only to see play turn on itself, disappear, return—snarling, breath heavy, gasping, bleeding dry again—with silence standing ready to accost the world above, the world below

the dam is broken, flood impends.

This space: not to speak of it, but to scratch in its dirt.

Disappearance.
Remnants.
Returns.

It has already reformed, and will again.

With this murder, the haunt has begun.

With this scratch, war has begun.

The Owl

owl of evisceration

(while the specter lacks witness)

(to haunt, yet to not see the one who enacts, replicates, transmutes
writing (scratching) as murder)

The owl hoots, fog aflame. Prophecy that bends, sways, to that
which has already happened and that which impends. Bending,
swaying, the graveyard's wind—bad air. Prophecy: a song, an echo
that pollutes.

At once a song and a call to arms.

After murder, the nude rattle of this call still resonates.

The owl's witness
(abandonment of accountability)
(humanity's absence, the inhuman gaze)
(elusion of meaning: murder as heinous as it is playful)
(the indifference of immediacy—to blink is to shutter
the owl captures the negative of thought;
the talon—a scratch, not of utter erasure
but manipulation of the negative)

In that lack of lapse, the witness becomes performer. The owl, called
into inexistence, trapped within the bad air of the graveyard—born
of its own prophetic cry that incites the cyclic reverberations of
blood lust.

The ground here is warm, but it is not young.

...wings quivering...

Death, exhausted...

(suffocated itself, it did not want you

...what, then, when the ghost is stirred by these chatters...

it too had a nest)

A witness, called into inexistence
gaze that tears at awareness, strips away the ritual
we can no longer see our disappearance
cannot feel it, live in it
the graveyard is burying itself, a sinkhole
a haunting that was not, will not be...

…seen by the owl, but not known

(cycles and repetitions)
(in this moment, to be the vestige)
(traces (of a species) that can be acted upon)

Murder, one of horror; performance of the murder, one that equalizes the echoes of the scream with the silence of the owl's gaze. The hoot, the prophecy, the song lingers, it affects its own operation.

One is pulled into becoming-trace, pays for being seen.

Damning, this lack of time.

The witness has stolen time needed by way of its inexistence; no one to follow, no one to watch. Each movement, each stroke, one of infinite sensation.

Traces are eviscerated

traces, spectral skin-mist, a new flesh

murder, one of speed

performance of the murder, one of inactivity

The owl lands on the shoulder
nibbles at the ear   with
each gesture of the beak, another trace disappears
as the talon sinks in—as it scratches—erasure.
Not an utter erasure, but a manipulation.
Traces of traces.

(a feather dipped in blood wells, an edict scrawled):

As you are scratched, you are erased.
As you are seen, you are not known.
The specter returns again
to not bear witness to the owl's witness,
to not witness this erasure.
There it hovers,
there it smolders.

Spectral Placements

(lack of burden: ecstatic horror,
noise and silence, muffled screams.
forward potentials, the haunting that is and will be again.
to be terrorized by reverberations
of one's gestures three steps ahead)

(lack of territory: erasure, razed ground, nameless tomb.
witness stolen by the owl; less a burial ground, more a lair)

(lack of clock: a murder and haunt always occurring.
the hand that stabs and the hand that falls limp.
the owl's song, an ode to the broken hourglass
and the cinders of parchment aflame)

Spectral Vantages

(lack of witness lends to the unseen.
to move across without sight, to wander,
to illicit veiled horror.
blind to those who cannot linger.
blind to the ash, to the smoke,
to the throats of those who cry out)

(lack of witness lends to the forgotten.
the haunt: birth of a god,
one willing to turn the blade on himself.
one who does not know why he is there,
nor why he is no longer there.
one who wonders why there are screams,
why there are no screams)

(lack of witness lends to the displaced.
no ground, no air.
to be suspended, fastened, yet floating, careening.
becoming the skin-mist, becoming the atmosphere.
flight and burial.
bastard resurrection)

The Graveyard (II.)

(the specter's gaze, empty as a mirror)

67

Haunting as penalty
(this razed ground runs across others
no longer above or below, but interwoven,
waste that scatters,
hidden from sight, though the vestiges bleed through)

(a penalty, if only to return again to pay)

the hand moves, another body falls

disappearance within oneself

to slip

stars of ice, fearing to shine

The graveyard, not what will be; rather what is and what must be. Weight: a dragging-down. Sky falling into earth, earth falling into fluid, fluid falling onto the skin-mist of the specter. Impossibility: the penalty of the epitaph—the naming—the scratching. The only law is compulsion.

The impossibility of restraint.

Architectonics

Of the...
Holes, Sands

The Hallway
What is Seen, What is Felt

The Space Beneath
What is Seen, What is Felt

Enclosures
The Closet, the Walls, the Floors

Imprisonment
The Cell, the Held-Down

-Reflection: Awareness of the image of anomaly, image of the hollow, the figure of nothing

-Reflection: Of the once-concealed...
    the nameless condition
    (illness of the unfamiliar, disease not of the self,
but of the absence of self—to unbound in the midst of this absence)

    -Unveiled
    (removal of the shroud, magnified imperfections)

    -To tear and puncture
    (sharpness/jaggedness, the edge)

- The breakable
(what was once roped together is now in   fragments)

-Transparency
(what is seen through the device of reflection, what is
    distant yet always
    alongside)
-Texture of the fragile
  (the continuous)

-Texture of the uneven
(the coarse)

-To be consumed by glass; taken in by the object that will reveal
(to be unmasked by the mask itself)

                              -This opening will consume.

   -This is the region of the far-off, the underlying;
            the place in which impulse remains and
                        impossibility no longer disturbs.
                              The vanishing of
            this disturbance allows one to
            recover in the aftermath of the collapse.
-This passage will lead one to cavernous realms. This territory is one
      of coldness, where the dismantled are embraced.

   -Here, there is erasure of the exhaustion caused
         by the ones who are risen. Here, only
                  remnants of the fallen remain.

         -This is the chasm of the shattered
   (shards of the old and obscene, pieces of the devastated)

   -Heard are the echoes of voices once
         stifled by hands of the
                        dull...hands covered in
                              the waste of excess.

                  -Inseparability
      (found within this: the seductive, the unbearable)

-Absence of expressions, or the presence of the inexpressible

-In this space, one becomes rid of the accidental,
         the irrelevant; strength is not wasted of
                        the undesired.

   -To discover the
                  undisturbed
                                    stretch
            (covering, the sheet)

      -Beckoning: to be drawn towards the
               chants of stillness

(slow lure)

-Movements of stillness, severity of an uprising
(summoned by the calm, awakened by the fever of grains)

-Barren space as a companion whose movements are manipulated
by one's desires
(when the desolate becomes the spectacle)
-Engraved on this surface are imprints of a wandering
(brought here by the allure of the unknown).

-From the depths, beneath stillness
(an emergence, disquiet)

-Collision of forces
(merging of

sand
and wind,
breaking of stillness)

-Debris and air entwined
(ceaseless struggle between stillness and delirium)

-Grains will slip through trembling fingers
(vulnerability).

-Narrowness

-That which is in-between: to exist
between points of extremity.
-Contours, crevices,
patterns
(discontinuous marks of the ancient and ruined)

-Endless constraint
(space becomes compressed as one walks down this path)

-Layers within, layers envelop
(to lose oneself amidst the levels, in the stories of the corridor)

-Smoothness along the floor
(smoothness as the source of
disorder,
this surface calls for one to imprint...to leave traces)
-Glare of the light above

(illumination will ingest)

-Broken portraits: to be surrounded by designs of the ones before
(architects of this entrapment are
within the walls, within the heaviness
felt by the one who goes this way.
This was once a sketch, this is now a
space abandoned by all but one)

-Gaze of the end seen from a
distance
(to recognize
the point one
will never reach)

-Not a willful entering, but a throwing-in (ice of a shove)

-Lowered when in this space (to be the one beneath)

-Hall in which only vanishing is promised
(one knows that nothing should be held because
everything will be taken)

-Submerged: to be soaked, then
seized (damp, in the mouth
of strangeness)

-Between strangling and embrace
(there is warmth in contempt)

-To be against, in the middle, never
above (depths)

-Heavy and embracing collapse (weight
on the
back of
the coward, to
surrender during night
of perishing and absence)

-Fatigue (empty, haggard)

-To accept this fate (first met with resistance, now embraced)

-For storage and control (switchboards, pipes)

-For the boxed-off: the unneeded and abandoned
      (buried, pushed aside, piled up, behind, in
      corners, under floorboards)

-The dust-covered and
            intentionally
                              hidden
            (the ancient, secrecy)

-Space of scratches, scribbling
            (the imperfect)

      -Dampness (leaks, webs)

      - The decrepit (negligence causing corrosion)

        - The unclean (filth causing corrosion)

          - Rough/concrete, cinder
            (the furnace, incineration)

  - Where the rats and insects
                        dwell
        (the ones who move too quickly)

      - Protection from disaster (transient shelter)

    -To be without air, restricted (crawl space, strangulation)

        -Formless presence (that which will taunt)

  -Fear (hiding place for the monster, the
                  haunted,
              nightmares)

      -To tremble, to panic (slow movements, paranoia)

          -Disturbing calm (silence as disturbance,
                    silence
                  like stone)

  -Concealment of bodies beneath the
                            boards

      -Paralysis

(moment of awe, endless weakening)

-Anxiety
(when one's greatest desire is to leave this place,
when one realizes that this place will never be left)

-The mess, the disorganized, the thrown-in
(accumulation, desertion, projection into forgotten space)

-Space as the thing that drenches
(swallowed one: to sink, to rest at
bottom)

-Stagnant yet
wandering (fastened:
stillness, staggering)

-Outline of something unnatural, something eroded
(disorientation caused by the unknown and vicious)

-To confront only that which will drain (this is a breaking-down,
a divesting and dousing of the form).
Felt is the grip of a presence
half-vanishing, half-steel;
the feeling of anguish in
being lowered
(the chasm into
which nothing falls).

-Entangled, pitted, to collapse
(in knots, hollowed, to burst while in the arms).
Grimace: to grow fond of imprisonment

-This space, unmoving, yet still able to bludgeon, to shove
(the perpetual throw)

-Violent and bright, both prolonged and
abrupt, the first and final blow
(birth and execution).

The light of
absence
resembles the light of the beginning and end.

-Hunger and blindness; blindness lifts and carries away...saves the
eyes, the mind.
Mind, the affliction.

-Closeness (familiarity with that which is blank and
without). Whiteness (sameness, purity, tedium).
These walls seek to subdue the delirious,
to pacify those whose minds
are deep within the
trenches.

-To
force
the noiseless to
respond: the cry, the call, the lure
(what is awakened? what does this surface summon?
the thing that beckons as the object of desire)

-Decoy: how can the one who is being deceived by space deceive
space
in turn?

-Separation (divisions, layers, thickness, what
supports but encloses). These walls
imprison; one is detached from
any absolute reality.

-Infestation, consumption, erosion
(ruined by the ones who were concealed, consumed by that which is
smaller.
To transcend size)

-Strength: that which is inexhaustible

-Dust (what has accumulated
over time, remains that
harm
the
body)

-Movements upon the floor, along the walls
(marks representing past steps)

-Knots, crevices, discontinuity (what is felt after the fall)

-What does it mean to be exposed and emptied by walls,
ground, ceiling, openings (removal/exposure)?
To carve marks on skin, on walls. To carve
escape through skin, through
walls

-Chewed by
space,
never
swallowed...but
to exist in the mouth
until one confronts the end
(to also exist in the eyes, between the
teeth, in the bones)

-Idleness as the aftermath of criminality
(once enlivened by the illicit...
once seduced and stricken by violation).
Rituals are created to distract oneself from what is being
experienced. One is amused by shadows of the inanimate, and
the shadow of
that which is animate yet
always
fading,
always being
drained.

-Condemned
(in the image of exclusion, in the posture of the one denied,
divided—in halls of the mind: calmness, gravel, outline of the one
below)

-Heaviness (weight of a dullness that wanders, a force
that reaches across and underneath, the weight of
nothing. To be absorbed then expelled by
this weight)

-Movement
(manipulated
movements of
the body and machine;
the body as a machine—coldness,
rust, reflections. To slip over—what slips
from the mind—loss of balance)

79

-Entrance

(space enters through openings created in the body—steals from
the body. The dive, unrelenting. One who is tormented becomes
                    eager for more
torment, awaits it, and calls for it.
                    Desperate one: dissolving in the
                                    center of a space too
                                                    horribly calm)

    -Dread (to replace dread with
                            acceptance, to no longer resist
                            the compression)

    -To exist only where one will be lowered, drenched, mocked

        -To be suffocated by the imaginary one, the heavy one

                -Young, withering, dust of youth
    (the one in mud, in thirst, in birth and death of a disaster)

    -In the walls of this night, the
                    holes of this night. Night,
                                    the swamp.

                                            Night,
                                                    the
                                            oppressor.
                                            Night, the
                    desired misfortune.
                                        Waste, nothing else

        -Needed and nauseous, whole but scattered.
        This is a struggle that is found underneath...
                one that goes across the neck, the eyes.

        -Sensation of bitterness, of life covered in idiots' slobber,
                                                of lacerations on
                            spirit and limbs.

    -This moment is one of viciousness;
                    when infancy and old age are
                                        entwined
            (to plunge into
                    the mud of

80

innocence and
guilt).

-What was once hesitation in the
throat is now
rapture
at the bottom of the lungs.

-This is rapid...like hanging, like demolition.

-Revival is found in devastation.

The Author—
Counter-Prayer
and The
Apocryphal

HERETIC—DOG

Suddenly appears, follows, overtakes

Blankness=youth; age and experience have nothing to set themselves in, nothing to grasp or carve; slick body, smooth mind
-as a result, the dog should desire to always die young; no old dog wants to live
-body as intersecting surfaces;
                              trembling the body are waves of air
-any flow over the body wraps close to the surface but can never penetrate a pore-less skin; they can never grow any hair

The Soft Tooth: every incision strikes at the nerve; eating is always painful

Nails/Claws: the anguish of their Uselessness

Ear (tinnitus): life cannot happen—other things just do not happen (when the world does not exist)

You can pull any surface to appear as from the inside

(urge, drive, hunt, pursue)

Always Hungry
Lyssa
Exquisite Terrain
Touch; the Force of Collision
Close to the Ground
From Below the Surface
Promise of the Depths
Suspension of Breath
At the Door; At the Foot of the Bed
(Whose?)(and Why?)
Running Circles
Somewhere is as Good as Anywhere
Why Here is Always a Somewhere
Prostration-Body Becomes Altar, Table

THE QUESTION OF BURNING

Process of conflagration

The turning of desire trussed within an utterance that more often than not devolves into a prayer or wish is as much hampered by the tethering with which it is harnessed as it is bolstered. Rotation begins on the formulations of a questioning or demand, but in order to propel itself forward and not dissipate within the airiness of prayer, it must be held into a position or posture to gather force.

Demand, Precariousness, Address—a Speaking-to, Cold Intimacy, Proximity

Whispering/working your way into Ears, schism—how structured prayer becomes wordless prayer—the personal prayer?—a seizing, a choosing, an insertion (promising to watch and to return)

Draws you out; gathers distance

When a prayer for you and to you is toward a corresponding obliteration

Destroys the myth that in a quiet world, life can be lived mute

Should never satiate or calm, but create a quiet desperation for more

Body as table/altar/stain

Yawn—Vanishings—Draught

Somehow events escape those who are ready

One never stays within his own company for very long

Question of inheritance: the heretical as the heir to the prayer; to mislead, the unorthodox creating an alternative to the prayer and the spell; the counter-prayer, the counter-spell; a quickening of desire, to render oneself permeable, as membrane amplifying desire.

The implications of prayer ultimately lead to heresy, in which the one who prays separates from desire and attaches to something other, interpreted as stronger or greater, gambling its life in an attempt to guarantee its existence. To convince the future that this desire was already an essential fabric. Prayer officially begins at the structural level, where the dictated words shrink the one who prays and allows entrance to an enclosed, imageless space, and from the continuation of structured prayer emerges the personal prayer (heretical prayer) that releases the author from its purpose.

MOTIONING BODY

(Worming your way into the Nonexistence that is denied you when
you are most ready for dissolution)

Prayers and spells provide a motioning body, a fulcrum upon which
to angle itself. One's connection to the shaping of a growing desire
springs from the hands, the feet, the head, the lungs, the belly, the
lines and figures drawn in space designed to amplify pulsations, and
to express nuances. The danger of this involvement is when the
connections become attachments, and the future life of desire is
compromised.

A heightened state that has the nose bleeding perpetually, a heady
altitude that displaces the air of the body, which must be occupied
in order to disappear while desire accumulates.

Body is conduit, vessel retwisting the fibers of reality; necessary to
the process

DIS-MANTELED

Structured prayer is ultimately meant to flatten, erase, dilute—a
freezing process that, through bareness, allows proximity to the
silence of being that takes form in the exaggerations and
malformations of god.

When conducting spells, the facilitator assumes the role of the
catalyst to an event, the moving figure that ultimately falls in the
way. The tools that necessarily accompany a spell indicate a kind of
clumsiness. In prayer, however, one has nothing to offer. There is no
exchange of blood. And every petition, provocation, glorification is
commenced in proximity of an undertow that will eventually claim
the direction of an unyielding craving. Both the mechanics of its
survival and the will of the supplicant require that desire be released
from its imprisoned state in order to be disencumbered.

In doing so, the one who performs prayer, then, reduces body and
presence through a process of Preoccupation and Compression, to
the function of a membrane whose permeability only acts as a
Quickening-Agent. Its release entails a complete loss of control for
the one who intercepted and malformed it. In this separation, the
supplicant cannot even rely on the Aptitude of the Skill applied, or
the belief that for the minor duration that desire was graspable,

infusion was able to occur. Unleashed, desire is allowed to undergo its own transformation of will, regardless of whether it still decides to take up its new inheritance or develop its own, the proof of which is only viewable in the outcome, and is not guaranteed a witness.

GERM/SHRINKAGE

Rudiment
Blind Inception

The strength of your will/desire to survive without you; desire can no longer belong to you or be known to you; all of its strength lies in its ability to fling itself forward; the potency of a prayer to insert itself imperceptibly, a concentration of accumulated will/desire into future reality's imageless Dream-Space; future will perceive it as its own impulse.

The real pleasure occurs in the momentary and vicarious possibility of writing the future despite itself. To accompany and accelerate a condensation, a Shrinkage that results in a Germ, able to not only float in and out of memory and dream, but to be able to penetrate that region where there is yet no discernable image, and to inscribe a suggestion that is no less fierce and all the more necessary for its size. Its density and material allow implantation to occur under the hand of an irresistible confusion, the kind that does not leave the day to itself. If not immediately borne to the forefront of any concentrated effort, it will be allowed to linger within that sensitive space for its perplexing innervation, even nursed to impel its own ushering.

IMAGELESS PLACE

The Topography of Elsewhere

The resulting amalgamation becomes, despite all the layering, the convergence of all these images, a crude inscription, an engraving whose primitiveness allows it to become imageless. In this imageless place, we are brought into the Floor/Canvas upon which all this has occurred, which could very well be the miniscus of our underlayering with which we have so little direct communication or command over. Images are made primitive when they are stripped down to their counter-muscles.

To denude by way of addition rather than subtraction is an inverted understanding of Nudity. The counter-muscles that lead to imagelessness reveal themselves through the image that is habitually being employed, that is put under siege. They are not present within the image as much as in the surrounding space, which appears to dislocate everything that is implanted within it. It is a space made blank by being unable to project anything particularized, dark by virtue of making everything it touches or everything placed upon it as obscure, excessive, needless and transportable. In seeming vacant by not excluding you or pushing you out, it is a writhing forest floor reaching in all directions, all the more heavy and disconcerting for being permeable and boundless.

Because entering and exiting such a space is easily interrupted just by looking, returning to a world that separates itself and is therefore filled with things (flagrant lapses that arrive could be speedily glossed over), it becomes evident that what one initiates with an image never ends with its features, though, initiated by them, they as much rein you in as usher you forward. Remembering to look at things and not be devoured by their images.

SPILLAGE

When counter-prayer enters the Public Spheres and Unwelcoming Arenas

The upheaval and tragedy that mark undoing cannot match the exacting ferocity of unfurling. Though the word houses delicate, breathy notions such as smoke, petals, sails and wings, it is not muted in acuteness, impact, nor expression through comely agents. The spreading, punctuated by the gentleness of a well-nourished mania, extends through soft rushes, past the event with which undoing localizes. When attempting to transfix a phenomenon, one must believe that he is trapped outside. Incorporation cannot be possible. The only avenue toward Convergence lies in the process of unfastening. The performance of the Destroyer culminates in an effortless transition from Destroyer to Redeemer, where the event is consummated in a spectacular ruination. Any remaining fragments are emptied of all possible dignity apart from that of littering the floor in ornamentation of what is when unmasked—indiscriminate hunger, the forgettability of the kill that has fallen to an uncultured Appetite. The Redeemer dreams of the moment in death when the crucial body is induced—rapture that will pierce its way into the central Somewhere. It is the accompanying Lyssa to this famishment that will not allow for multiple deaths, but the same death that is reduced until all that could have suggested or fostered repose is cut away. Unfurling does not begin with the stalking of a phenomenon; it is first seen as a withdrawal. Repose begins with an abandonment of the world, where incredible distance allows the outside to disappear while maintaining the position of residing, inhabiting. There is just an inside. The recumbent gather themselves in a knot in order to attain the peace that allows for rest. When planted into position, and body solidifies into nothingness (a rock- becoming), all inhibition and resistance fall. Out of themselves, the recumbent find that they are in a place without location, an Elsewhere through which one travels, an occupation of drift work. There is no settling into an image that does not shift. Loss of gravity disassembles all phenomena into an expanding reverie that reaches beyond the transfixed points with which some attempt to achieve a stranglehold on the significance of an occurrence, into the deterritorialized space of the imagination, into which access is gained through a willingness to disregard the promise of an essential relevance.

SHROUD: FROM THE INSIDE

(embracing, taking shapes, concealment,
constructing temporary Insides from which to draw)

The re-experiencing of persons and things gives them a body that extends beyond the colors, shapes, substances and dimensions that are perceived outside of the Imaginal rendering. An imagined entity is a gutted, re-situated building that emerges out of a blurred landscape, standing alone. Outlines and countenance are shifted with the smear of double vision, and though certain details are kept (and malformed), the swollen actuality is found divorcing it from knowable measurements. Without the cohesive assurance of exactitude, anything that is reassembled in the dark is done so according to the Blueprint of lingering impressions. Its articulations formed with an intuitive understanding of collapsibility. How it folds back determines its reappearance within the sphere in which it was conjured. To remain indelible, the House must rely on certain attributes gained by becoming through decompression—a moving picture.

The realization is made that there is no separating the construction of the House from its physicality. Body and body, one being perceived as being on the outside. another on the in, but there can be no tracing of one without experiencing the contours of the other. Image as body is recognizable despite complete Flatness. Flatness that does not signify a lack of depth, but depth without the gravitational pull downward, verticality-without-height. A Flatness that allows the components of the image to glide over and away from each other. Here, body is not being contrasted with soul. The compartment, such as the House, is always being built, and always under the quiet assumption that this is the one that you will keep.

After, however, its disappearance, when the thought of it has passed, it can never be reclaimed as it was the moment before, frozen as it seemed to be in thought. When disappearing, it takes with it part of the canvas from which it had emerged, slowly building its own raft.

Although the image is always being removed through a process of superimposing, pieces remain that escape removal and coalesce with other surviving elements. What remains is a skeletal structure that reinforces itself by relying on having few basic members at a time in order to persevere, none of which is irreplaceable. What allows the House as thought to have a sufficiently reliable skeletal structure, one that survives its constant effacement, is the fact that most of the Houses with which an individual becomes acquainted throughout life share distinct anatomic similarities. Nevertheless this constant superimposing of images generates a peeling that does not stop unless the construction stops, unless the House is not only made completely extinct from memory and future but unmade in entirety. The House must become an unthinkable notion.

SUBMERGENCE: DROWING ON DRY LAND

(to be swallowed up, being forced to drink, driving out, overwhelm, being compelled to walk while one slowly drowns, is this body of water particular to each individual? the swelling lung, the body becoming an Unreachable Shore)

Without heart. Out of the heart, and yet always on the heart's behalf. This contraption has been devised to manufacture the delicate sensitivity that often initiates vitalism that is necessary to keep it alive. It is where intricacy, fragility, and unnatural tenacity combine to produce unusual instances of sustenance that reorient an appetite.

    -If *true*, a heart is able to produce in any environment—an unfurling sense of home. This home promises a stronghold, and yet it strands you. Against every healthy instinct the heart's passenger can easily be nestled in the depths of a crumbling ocean. What the heart seeks is not to preserve *you* as much as itself, suggesting that its life is not tied to that of its host.

-The heart becomes a foreign agent, and at times conspires against even one's deep wishes and desires. It does not give what is perceived as essential; when it succeeds in destroying lives for you that were held dear and imperative, it demands that you confront as that which it has never been—a hardy piece of plumbing.

FRENETICISM: INFLAMMATION OF THE BRAIN

Blood lessens into water, contributing to its Thirst

There is no possibility for speaking directly to god/source/the totality of reality; there is no possibility for response, or rather of knowing from where it came...or its actual meaning; rather, the possibility that an unknown god/entity may answer in another/ciphered language—a misinterpreted word.

Always immediate. Cannot be relived or continued. There is no continuing the same prayer, yet it is never finished; the challenge is to pour as much potency into it before it dissipates. Elongating prayer into a counter-prayer is a suspension of breath.

Collection

The following consists of a catalogue of collection-modalities. The objects under consideration will be designated in terms of their respective collectors, the impulses to gather them, the methods of attainment, the arrangements of their forms (for display), the instruments of retrieval, the locations of encounter, the rarity of the possession, and the descriptive powers therein. What is the distinguishing characteristic that spellbinds the collector (and renders motionless)?

To catalogue is to seek that which is "not completely defined," a certain research and awareness of potential, drawn-through by an unknown, accountable instinct. The catalogue is the site of tonic, of what darkens with exposure, of astringents and things kept with great care. Alarming after- effects may occur. The catalogue is a practice of inhalation, a crystallized, medicated cane; one thinks of medicinally impregnated sugar cubes (unassuming). The catalogue holds what is insoluble in boiling water (cannot adapt to new textures), what is slightly bitter in taste (sedation-hysteria), what is dangerous to the eyes, what is not to be held by open flame (begins to decompose and vaporize). It is a dose: antidote.

To collect is to enter into a space where one knows one is being watched—to seek the softened—the space where one has already been. It is to stumble along the similar path—fall just outside the designated home—its own preservation of the dissimilar. One thinks of the box: the cruelty/murder through deprivation (starvation); the isolated (caged); the neglected (pale); the object of interest. To be strung and worn around one's neck (forced to choke).

There are many: the crowds, the consumer, the mythological, those who need to collect in order to survive. There are authorized forms of collecting (things that are allowed) and unauthorized forms (things that must never be taken). What would be the third collector?

And what does one seek? All items become prospective collectables: shards of colored glass, poorly written myths, sinners, frothed blood, stones with black string, skins, wall linings, miniatures, flavored salts, industrial copper wire, teeth, imperfections (scars...handicaps... speech...), rusted locks, stitches, microbes, parasites, passageways. The collection is itself a permitted mode of transgression, where residence is impossible.

7.1

7.1.1 **Object**: Hides/Bones

7.1.2 **Collector**: The Hunter

7.1.3 **Impulse**: Mercilessness

7.1.4 **Methodology**: Apprehension (overtaking, overpowering, passing through)

7.1.5 **Arrangement**: Mounted (to display in honor, to collect only the head)

7.1.6 **Instrument**: Rope

7.1.7 **Location**: Forest

7.1.8 **Description:** To catch the object: against choice of self and desire—the quiet and calm of silence—the almost-accessed collectible— pursue/grub/divine-scour/grope/dredge/fumble/drag—leave no stone unturned—the bottom of a body of water—locate and discover existence unsloped/steep/upright/ abrupt; the mortal-earthborn

7.2

7.2.1 **Object**: Side-Effects/Reactions/Infections

7.2.2 **Collector**: The Sickly

7.2.3 **Impulse**: Leniency (trust toward substance)

7.2.4 **Methodology**: Obsession (to scrutinize and treat variations)

7.2.5 **Arrangement**: Mass (magnitude of the pill)

7.2.6 **Instrument**: Extracts (those that are only attainable from white needles)

7.2.7 **Location**: Bedridden

7.2.8 **Description**: Without caution or precision, the ill swallow the heaping, colorful vision of future health—Death (permanent implication)—experience of interrupted misfortunes (weary)—to make "being" an object—the vehicle of fixation—the fomite: the carrier

7.3

7.3.1 **Object**: Smoke

7.3.2 **Collector**: The Addict

7.3.3 **Impulse**: Strain (to deplete one's stash, the always-seeking)

7.3.4 **Methodology**: Floating (to fill cavities)

7.3.5 **Arrangement**: Lined (on glass, in plastic, encased with paper)

7.3.6 **Instrument**: Veins

7.3.7 **Location**: Alleyway

7.3.8   **Description**: To contact a series of undesirables/misfits/monsters—impossible attempt to go unseen—to lick the surface of any particle reminiscence—unearthen charms—wet mouth and pointed eyes—granulated—increasing through hands (quick, breathless)—snatches—separating lumps—the drug (causes the pupil of the eye to dilate)—frailty—obsolete instruments (without fetish or value)—cycle of obsolescence and renewal—to dedicate one's life to human flaw—excise—removal by cutting out (to seek the object through fluids)—the *roué*—interested only in blood of a certain texture: that which foams (a thickness that draws dense, behind the free-flowing)

7.4

7.4.1   **Object**: Debris
7.4.2   **Collector**: The Vagrant
7.4.3   **Impulse**: Damnation (punishment)
7.4.4   **Methodology**: Begging (transfer guilt, extend the arms, look to the ground)
7.4.5   **Arrangement**: Sheets (corners tied)
7.4.6   **Instrument**: Hands
7.4.7   **Location**: Viaduct
7.4.8   **Description**: The vagabond—the anti-collector (the most entranced)—the wanderer. Is the one who roams the most specific of collectors, or is this the character who experiences the lost objects of devotion? What does the vagrant keep in its satchel? The one that collects only what is necessary—what is the mode of interaction between the collector and the collected when everything needs a function? Pushed away v. moving towards. Is this the recognized seeker, or the exiled? Inertia (the gypsy)

7.5

7.5.1   **Object**: Anti-Genealogies
7.5.2   **Collector**: The Half-Breed
7.5.3   **Impulse**: Gathering (only what would benefit the cultureless)
7.5.4   **Methodology**: Precipitous (to hasten, lacking the due fixation)
7.5.5   **Arrangement**: Levels (the superficial interests)
7.5.6   **Instrument**: Inheritance (heirloom infatuation)
7.5.7   **Location**: Suburban: the safe collector—without understanding—only in the disjoined past

7.5.8   **Description**: To become sterilized (removal of history)—
how does one organize the objects/rituals/
languages/customs of partial cultures? What becomes
sacred? What is the fascination? To become embedded in
a culture that has nothing to do with you—what is
collected when one abandons history? Disgust of
representations—to divorce oneself of all objects...what is
it to be without? Fashionable novelty—hereditary—
through death, the miniatures built inside the bottles: the
pirate ship

7.6
7.6.1   **Object**: Ash
7.6.2   **Collector**: The Arsonist
7.6.3   **Impulse**: Exposure (*esprit*: vivacious and clever)
7.6.4   **Methodology**: Ignition (to smolder, combust, burn)
7.6.5   **Arrangement**: Piles (lack of movement, lack of attention to
temperature)
7.6.6   **Instrument**: Flint (overgrown)
7.6.7   **Location**: Positioned in the sun
7.6.8   **Description**: To come before the ash—to hold the
potential of warmth, when the collector becomes
reckless—an inattentiveness to the object—friction: too
many, melting, gaining ground, obtain sulfur from the
fires—this immobility causes man-made death

7.7
7.7.1   **Object**: Discardings (collection of the unwanted)
7.7.2   **Collector**: The Antiquarian
7.7.3   **Impulse**: Clasping (desperation)
7.7.4   **Methodology**: Trade (the bargainer)
7.7.5   **Arrangement**: Lots (curiosity, formation, groupings)
7.7.6   **Instrument**: Taste (style: selective v. accepting)
7.7.7   **Location**: Adjacent Worlds (after total confiscation)
7.7.8   **Description**: The dealer (temporary collector)—antiquity
(time)/survival (history)/economy (memories)/luxury
(stories)—association: the ability to keep the collectable
until the right time—fear of negligence: to overlook...skip
the ultimate (catch them all)...what was missed—to
collect the things around the object once it has been
exhausted—the flawless, the intact, the refined—similar
position of the hoarder: the one who seeks the
disinherited, the forgotten—to find significance and
necessary additions to buildups: a piece of cloth left over
after the rest has been used or sold—to find something

unusual in the throwaways...worth the assumed, future
necessity

7.8
7.8.1 **Object**: Debts
7.8.2 **Collector**: The Thief
7.8.3 **Impulse**: Pillage (raid, harass, belittle, waste, sacrifice)
7.8.4 **Methodology**: Confiscation (deprivation)
7.8.5 **Arrangement**: Concealed (non-visual species)
7.8.6 **Instrument**: Intimidation (careless)
7.8.7 **Location**: Undisclosed (provisional)
7.8.8 **Description**: Criminality: become miniscule (not
fragmented), small enough to gain access anywhere; to go
undetected—glyptic concerns, or carvings, engravings of
the careless collector—worth: the other (the subjective
worth)—beguile: the cheat...force and impose
deceit...deprivation... piracy—the ruler: force—
rebellion...earns profits

7.9
7.9.1 **Object**: Folklore
7.9.2 **Collector**: The Story Teller
7.9.3 **Impulse**: Memory (unpacking, disband, selected
components)
7.9.4 **Methodology**: Games (role-play, tokenization)
7.9.5 **Arrangement**: Coils (spiraled, twisted, looped, rotated,
circular, ringed, turned, confused)
7.9.6 **Instrument**: Riddles (conundrums)
7.9.7 **Location**: Just Outside (leaning to the right and above)
7.9.8 **Description**: The creation of a break: multiple ends,
multiple deaths—to be born, to birth oneself—to cradle,
and rediscover the childish (fallacy, fables, and fairy
tales)—the delusions of misinformed legends,
determination that encourages discomfort, groveling—
forcefully encourage (implant/imbue)—acting as Impasto,
or ornamental wire—formed into delicate tracery
(interlacing)—the raconteur dresses its tales in metaphor
and coats the importance in theatrics and illustration

7.10
7.10.1 **Object**: Bewilderment
7.10.2 **Collector**: The Psychic
7.10.3 **Impulse**: Instinct (to see what is not necessarily present)
7.10.4 **Methodology**: Hiding (to compile, amass, accumulate,
make useful what is assumed)

7.10.5 **Arrangement**: Separation (to assign objects a future: the pre-mapped)

7.10.6 **Instrument**: *Memento-Mori*: objects kept to remind of the inevitability of death

7.10.7 **Location**: Cellar (the underground of an inconspicuous home)

7.10.8 **Description**: When one does not possess what is sought, the ones distinguished from the heavens will lead (through candlelit overgrown gardens, to rooms of ruby drapery and cloaked figurines lined with rows of selected quartz and stone)—to motivate, prompt, incite and instigate the incorrect findings—with cognitive impacts they speak of the destination (purpose) for the ones who find themselves astray—the marking of the seer: glossed eyes/tired hands/ moistened skin—perfumed in sage and rosemary

7.11
7.11.1 **Object**: Manufactured Intimacies
7.11.2 **Collector**: The Stalker
7.11.3 **Impulse**: Worship (to obtain anything associated)
7.11.4 **Methodology**: Curiosity (unease of wanting more knowledge)
7.11.5 **Arrangement**: Following (any distance: near and far)
7.11.6 **Instrument**: Charms (seduction, trance, enamor, captivation)
7.11.7 **Location**: Fantasy
7.11.8 **Description**: The observer: to see what is not meant to be visible, that which is not collected, but kept—the narrative of a Romantic collector—the justifications of the unclean collector—the ornate dreams, the ideal, metonymic, the unsent love letters—fixation: the poetry—parable: the imagery of the lyrical (the pseudo-exotic)—carries/covets (the personally valuable): locks of hair/tiles/souvenirs (the relics)

7.12
7.12.1 **Object**: Spider Webs (perceptible invisibility)
7.12.2 **Collector**: The Phantom
7.12.3 **Impulse**: Protection (this is the posture of what will be called "The Guardian")
7.12.4 **Methodology**: Signals (suspension)
7.12.5 **Arrangement**: Languid (listless and drooped)
7.12.6 **Instrument**: Netting (many kinds of disappearances must be used on the invisibles)

7.12.7 **Location**: Insomniacs' Dream-World (yellow discoloration of a tar-stained wall)

7.12.8 **Description**: Through tempered modes of resistance, the shadow shields the doomed from forgotten memories (repression), in states of non-reality and wishing (hope), and the hourglass (time)—three sections of the trunk, divided—white string-like masses form on tubing— spreads (increases underground, contagious)—connects with tubing of similar dividends—final scope: a white cord tangled between rock and dirt eventually severs all connection of elements—difficulty of freezing the ones who lack liquid/skin—what led the invisibles to seek the metal? Promise of eternal warmth—encased (armored)— given form—they since have burned

7.13

7.13.1 **Object**: Oddments

7.13.2 **Collector**: The Curator

7.13.3 **Impulse**: Covering (protection of lost valuables)

7.13.4 **Methodology**: Tribute (to the object)

7.13.5 **Arrangement**: Displacement (once removed from the original space)

7.13.6 **Instrument**: Eye/Vision (recognition of the peculiarity, talent, phenomenon: to create the experience of coming trends)

7.13.7 **Location**: The Showcase (the installation processes, the layered, the stacked, parallax: position of object differs from the viewpoint)

7.13.8 **Description**: Occurrences of Preservations: *The Pre, The Current*, and *The Yet-To-Come*—the prodigy becomes the malleable—human design—the curator becomes the draftsman (conniving, based on artifice; the lines of disloyalty form a brittle, arthritic terrace)—one who trains the potential: ruses/tricks/maneuvers—practices of deception (as art). Is the prodigy devoted to the craft or to the one most educated in the skill (guilt for the granted designation)? Techniques/expertise/abilities/ dexterity/agility/nimbleness (the clumsiness of a trainer without recognition of outshining and surpassing of the doubtful)—the master (the left- behind): one who stumbles upon those with talent—discovery of disrespect (necessity of the strange/oddity of the bland/astonishment of the under-defined)

For those who recognize: the coach (drills: creates the competitive, the bloodthirsty)—the professor (lectures/commands understanding/attainable by rote/to learn by heart)—the warden (enhancement through captivity/dispossession of harassments/ drained)—the supervisor—the keeper—the judge—creation of the trite man—the submissive—hatred of aptitude (pitied luminary), rejection of strength—the hated, unwanted collectable, those which should not be allowed out of their cages (fear of vengeance/retribution/a settling of scores)— those who display a proficiency become the bothered, the itchy, the dysfunctional and the lacking—without complete function

7.14

7.14.1 **Object**: Vials (filled with sand and dust)

7.14.2 **Collector**: The Blind

7.14.3 **Impulse**: Optic Radiation (what feels worthwhile: tactual hysteria)

7.14.4 **Methodology**: Defilement (what was never sacred; only when it is modified does one recognize the original's impermanence)

7.14.5 **Arrangement**: Isolated (apart from nerves, to camouflage the object's sensations)

7.14.6 **Instrument**: Cane (antennae, located by sensation on the tips of the fingers: precision is a necessity in this form of accumulating and separating such minuscule fragments of rock)

7.14.7 **Location**: Cylinder-Shaped Recesses

7.14.8 **Description**: Sand: eroded limestone, granite, feldspar, lava, magnetite, volcanic obsidian. Dust: textile fibers, paper fibers, pollen, soil and minerals, skin cells, hair, chalk. Color (sand): white, black, red, gold, light pink. Color (dust): grey, brown, white. Texture (sand): coarse, pebbled, cracked, bumpy, ribbed, gritty, smooth, glossy, grainy, powdery, fine, floury, mealy, hard. Texture (dust): spongy, silky, napped, stringy. Taste (sand): salt, nutty, smoky, sour. Taste (dust): flat, clotted. Reaction: accelerated sensation. Signs: texture/ brail/"caution hot." Sensation of the eye (pushed from behind). Sight: circular surroundings—centered wall of blood—the floor of the flooded: sloping downward and forward, the structure creates rapid and forceful descent, becoming inundated (land). Sight: image propelled forward through the carved-out (cavity), forming prominenus—not passing through as needed for perception of image; instead, it runs into the flood floor, diverted to the opposite wall-lining and imprinted onto the opposite ground, unable to be seen— permanent aching (subsequently, the image is lost to sight). Uses: occupy, interest, provoke the senses, make use of one's hand, training of recognition and particularity. Treats: idleness, headache, boredom, fever, peripheral breaks and detachment, pigment disturbances, distortion, general malaise, vomiting. Dose: daily therapy necessary, often in large amount to receive quick results. Interactions: keep away from healthy ocular receptors; dangerous absorption may occur

7.15

7.15.1 **Object**: Figments

7.15.2 **Collector**: Author

7.15.3 **Impulse**: Take/Distort/Abandon (ownership of the original idea; betrayal of beginnings)

7.15.4 **Methodology**: Peculiarity (specific understanding of unique quality: collectible-consumption)

7.15.5 **Arrangement**: Placements (texts, to stay in the correct place, to be the repeated word, to use the same ideas)

7.15.6 **Instrument**: Preferred (ballpoint pen, pencil, fountain, feather, chalk, crayons, paper, type, font, written word, language, representations, forms, names, invention, composition, understanding, infatuation, malformations, simplicity, complexity, ornamental ribbons of tenor)

7.15.7 **Location**: Hideaways/The Den/Library/Study: remote rooms with a table and lamp (where one can be intentionally secluded); walls lined in publications: volumes/journals/ledgers/ encyclopedias/ thesauruses/ dictionaries astrological/rhyming/conceptual/ maximizing/ minimizing/phonetic/picture/biographical/ multilingual/defining/scripts/registers/assemblages of alphabets and punctuations; the printed: where the idea can be borrowed but is meant to be returned; rooms filled with substances that have not yet been exhausted, where one feels small in comparison and traps oneself (capsulated and besieged) by the constructions/notions/ opinions of superiors

7.15.8 **Description:** The reader and the re-read—the creator, the object, (once collected, the collector kills the creator)—the craftsman—the poet—the interpreter and the interpreted. Textured cognition: uneven, irregular, cratered, soaked, asymmetrical, glassed, slippery,

dehydrated, calloused, brittle, thickened, fibrous, porous, dull, chromed, marbled. Flavors of intellect: delicate. Experiences of discernment: obsession, alienation, loss, misunderstanding, competitive tendencies, mental distress, abnormal emergence, morbid enlargement of limbs, resignation, acceptance of desire and inevitability, declension, unattainable pattern of thought, recklessness, madness, paranoia, aggression, deception, repression, obscurity, ideologies, punishment, excitation, entrapment, distraction, confusion, absurdity, mutation, extinction, revelations, originality, exhilaration, despair, disenchantment, nightmare, deprivation, suspicion—use
v. intention, potentiality (time), what can be learned but rarely is—consumption (numbers/quantity): to have the most unread books—the memorized meditations, prayers, mantras (immersion)—to penetrate (perforate)—provide the author with an ancillary (tools for support), impose urgency through memory (solicit difference)—disparateness (utter dissimilarity

Artificiality

I.
INTERPLAY

This is a writing of artificial interplay,
of the commingled, but never-touching...
Here words must indicate closeness (summoned),
though breaking thought from movement...
And this inscription creates the inauthentic, as a lapse,
as a multiple: to take oneself and create sheets/layers that
deviate slightly from the original...

This is a writing of performance,
of the show, in its own theater...
Here words must become a rehearsed-improvisation...
And this inscription marks
the super-reality, and the micro-reality
(to create the illusion of seeing the real)...

This is a writing of the threshold
(and what is the threshold? where is the threshold?),
the barrier, surpassing: flat ground—roundness—
vast spaces—plunged—thrown—pulled—
pierced and hanged—drained...
Here words accept the cost of passing lines,
the cost of keeping apart the entity...
And this inscription is of irreversible processes, the point at which
one cannot turn back, without metempsychosis,
rebirth of the soul, recycled...

This is a writing of separation, one that alienates the others...
Here words must arrive untied,
A trifurcation (divided into thirds)...
And this inscription parts without alliance, only traces
(shadows/detections/hints), produced by wear...

This is a writing of holes: rifts—chasms—scissures—crevices—
cracks—pockets—compartments—cavities—pores—
pits—hollows—tunnels (the opening)...
Here words puncture, become splinters (fragments)...
And this inscription will become
the means of access (to abnormality)...

This is a writing of quicksand,

106

one of seduction (magnetizes, pulls downward)...
Here writing dedicates itself to
the one it traps, the mesmerized...
And this inscription swallows whole, pardons none,
creates an inventory (accumulation/collection/combination)
of the fascinated...

This is a writing of blisters,
from the friction of imperfections (defects/flaws)...
Here words swell from resistance (vesicate/tumefy)...
And this inscription will produce an expansion,
a bloating (abscesses/boils)...

II.
MOVEMENT

This is a writing of transportation, toward
the interchangeable (liquidity), liquid automaticity,
liquid instantaneity...
Here words become a gesture (speed/actions),
though the challenge is to remain stable within,
to keep from slipping...
And this inscription is a curiosity—
false, engineered: to become the character
of the body inspired...

This is a writing of skin pressed to skin,
of minuscule sensitivity...
Here words bring about pinching, momentary movements
toward anxiety (paralysis/the race)...
And this inscription illuminates the nerves,
blankets them before they are seen...

III.
SENSATION

This is a writing of shared sensation (tongue/material/scars),
training the body to follow (ahead or behind)...
Here words fall beyond pain and pleasure to
vibrations from laughter, to shaking—trembling—

heat—nausea—heaviness...
And this inscription is its own approaching (allowance/defiance)...
This is a writing of suffocation,
imitating the shape and size of lungs...
Here words are covered in hives, seeking a reaction that causes:
the heart to race/stridor (to become blue/
loss of consciousness)...
And this inscription is one of panting/gasps,
one that changes skin's texture, one that causes an itch,
one that pollutes the air...

IV.
TIME

This is a writing of interruptions,
the pharmacological measure of a dose,
to overdose history/meteorology/war/
the future/the waters...
what does an overdosed future look like?...
Here word prove something:
that the future is to be erratic/
without inhibition/stumbling and blushed...
And this inscription is its own new sobriety,
one of the tranquilized society: altered, reconnected...

This is a writing of imperceptible whisperings/cries,
those of delicate difference (the unseen)...
Here words become an environmental adjustment (recognition);
one is taught not to listen for the haunting,
but to listen for the outcry
of the ones it has already passed...
And this inscription is a quick silence (a turning)
from a settling of sands...

This is a writing of numbness (the mutant memory),
against nostalgia...
Here words lean toward mortification:
to petrify/turning-stone, as an excess (to over-remember destroys,
to under-remember conceals,
allowing it to plan and perform an attack)...
And this inscription has this task: to steal a memory,
cripple it, replace its limbs with objects
(wood/cement/metal/ropes)

then place them back, allow a disturbance…
(there is no other exit for the memory…
it is in this forgetting that it gains strength,
is allowed to over-indulge)…

V.
TECHNIQUE

This is a writing of false ritual
(the misspoken incantation/the backwards spell),
mocked representations (imitations)…
Here words find placement in the erroneous
(the invalid/the wanderer)…
And this inscription reconstructs legibility fabricated)…
What orders and spacing exist now?
What offbeat anticipation of the page?

This is a writing of degeneration
(to lose the quality of the image),
the player piano, the Xerox (the partial/off the original)…
Here words generate the surrogate (clones),
the un-rooted offspring and the mirror
(reflection/refraction)…
And this inscription brings its own proximity,
its own freedom (entrapment), where duplications/copies
no longer need the other (the prewritten)…

This is a writing of temporary murders:
to continually commit miniscule suicides (strands of re-growth)…
Here words are internal suicides/mute screams (a shuddering)…
the ends: to complete the relationship with the other…
the death: to kill that which is created…
And this inscription asks:
what remains after one's "partial death?"
what is the technique one uses in a "partial suicide?"
what technique of regeneration/sacrifice?

This is a writing of consumption,
the groan of an overfed belly (a stillness)…
Here words are processes of absorption,
a constant ability to take in substance,
to catch what should never be caught…
And this inscription is one of surrender (the lover),

where the sound of the cry alone melts glass
(how does one trap the un-fleshed being?)...

VI.

BODY

This is a writing of malformation,
The transmission of a message,
one that offends, that brings wreckage,
one that transfers between the layers (tears)...
Here words accompany, as the dialect of a passenger
(to follow until delay), until entering exhaustion (to forget a layer),
leaving a silence that causes
one to know that one has been made deaf...
And this inscription is its own unmasking,
born of the absurdity (ability) to summon, without recognition,
that one is being stripped...

This is a writing of artificial bodies, of the accretion of organs,
of the body as mechanism and apparatus...
Here language becomes a physical series (spots and residues)
of altered states and miniscule differences,
of blood (escape from coldness)
and bloodlessness (loss of symbolic life)...
And this inscription is more a question of complexion
(heat/burning/melting/sickness/paleness),
attentive to texture (goose-flesh: fear, awe),
to the rash caused by infestation,
and to the expression of one within finite death (sleep)...

This is a writing of trace,
integrating both snakes and suffocation...
Here language becomes a technique of the nearsighted,
one that brings into view remains (bruises/scratches)
and the keloid (reactions/wounds)...
And this inscription is its own escape:
to wrap one's self in other skins,
to cloak in flesh in order to protect the calves,
for the false skin allows escape...

VII.
IDENTITY

This is a writing of mutiny (to become the artificial self),
where identification is forced to the surface
(to call out a demon) by endless means:
to become one of many (crowded),
to become dispossessed of oneself (transferred ownership),
to become distinctly different from oneself (unknowing),
to become indistinct from oneself
(lacking control, without form/outlines),
to become vague (to lose character),
to become visible or hidden (transparency v. opacity),
to become of adjusted senses (pleasure/pain),
to become the split (withdrawal/schism)...
Here language allows for a becoming-synthetic (man-made-man):
staged—painted—counterfeit—unreal—deceptive—
imaginary—hallucinatory (substances)...
And this inscription assigns the overdose
(to become drenched in self: to read one's own palms)...

Book II.

5.1

To make mediocre and to eliminate extremes. This is the world's mode of smoothing. It is done out of a vulnerability that conceals, a weakness that protects, a desperation that stagnates. Its function is to pull anything that lies at extreme boundaries into the middle ground, the safe-zone of thought.

This apparatus' method is to commit unthinkable acts of violence in ways that are so smooth as to be undetected. To willingly subject oneself to all possibilities is symptomatic of a strength grounded in one's other-worldliness and untouchability. To tolerate and permit is a weak, authoritative gesture whereby dangerous thoughts are adopted in diluted, domesticated forms. Those that tolerate tend to integrate new arrivals into an existing framework, in a method of homogenization. A reality that can only absorb anything that might arise must operate in such a manner as this. The criterion of any valuable principle: that it accelerates and amplifies dangerous thought. This machine will smooth over this failure, leveling everything and everyone, leaving them all with an identical dead-gaze and eliminating all difference between them.

7.1

CITIES

Built To Conceal
Circulation
(people—schedule—comfort)
To Seek The Everyday
(conformity—the uniform)
...The Consent For Solitude...
...To Seek The Solitude...
...Haunted By Bodies...
Suspension (buildings)
Swarms (heat)
The Infections (proximity)
Time (the clock) (the schedule)
...to form patterns of the other's time—
to accept the other's time...
Solitude/Altitude (unreachable)
...to build into the sky, to align with the gods...
Solitude from Ground (unseen)
Claustrophobia (the crowds: to fall amongst the common)

The View of Tomorrow
...to view the city from above the skyline...
...where you can look down upon everything ...
...to get the first glimpse of day...
...to seek solitude—to be forced into solitude...
...the pavement/the grid...to follow the grid...
...to become miniscule where everything is built up...
...to be at the top of the tallest and become unseen...
...to be the most visible at the bottom...
...to become the material...(to become unseen—
become the concrete, become the glass, become the steel)...
...to wear the shades of the city...(grey, white, black)...
...to make the city...to make earth in the city...
(parks, trees, gardens, zoos, lakes, beaches)

Travel Within the Earth
(the underground—the subway)
carved-out spaces (tunnels)
closeness to the underworld (the freaks, the monsters)
to align with the demons
(to dig, to remain untouched)

Avoid Darkness (street lights)
Noises (comfort in the noise, suspicious of silence)
Invisibility (always looked at, always watched,
always looking...)

Neutral (the cement skin that layers the dirt)
Unnatural Layers (smoothness, the drought)

Coldness—Glass—Steel—Concrete
(reflecting metal) (blackened glass)
...creating shadows to ensure the soul...
(buildings without shadows)
Grey (to absorb all colors—
to turn everything different shades)
Reflection—Visibility—Rumination
(to vomit—emesis—disgorgement)
Evidence (the glare—to become luminescent)

The Artist
...to steal the grey—to violate...
(to distort the distorted)
...to make pulse what was created dead ...

116

(defile, sacrifice)
...to become the carrier of color...
...to become the displaced (to displace)...
...to bother the ones in uniform...
...to show the city the color green...

6.1

Not a perfect smoothness, but a filing-down.

Recognized are chasms, breaches of sensation and perception, the backwards hand of the clock, ruptures of beauty (beautiful ruptures), breaks in lineage, in linearity, the shadow of a child's tear, fractures in a sea of ice (fractal light): all flaws, the deepening lines of imbrication, though forced to be trenches. Holes will be torn the moment before continuity cements.

They asked for sameness, they will be given smoothness.

The filing down, an exercise of speed. Hastening. Horizon bleeds through, structures must be leveled. Structures fall down in ash, nothing left standing. They asked for sameness, they will be given smoothness—and with it abrogation.

The faster one moves across you, the more one takes.

Currents (counter-currents, undercurrents), spectral empires running alongside this wasting horde, as present as they are undetectable, executing asperous modalities of their disappearances—disappearing within themselves, to the very unnaming of their impossible workings. To become these currents, to disappear within oneself, to move alongside the wasting horde in spectral paroxysms, to file down with unknowable velocity—

they asked for sameness, they will be given smoothness.

7.1.2

Stillness. The dead water—where death and those dying are left along the edges, where nothing crashes. Those who float on the still water are the ones who sink quickly, are grabbed by the weeds, chewed and digested by the soaked residual soil. This is where those who fight the rapids and lose are pushed to the sides—the quick, jagged water has no interest in the ones that cease creating waves. Before this moment, when the water still teases—at the point just before exhaustion—they look out in the middle of the rapid and see a space of smoothness...a pillow in the center of the turning whiteness. One dreams of refuge, safety, the calm accommodating waters and will attempt to position a landing on this soft current. Unwelcomed by the drifting form, one becomes aware of the deception, a trick played by the sun and the rapids—a reflection of further waters; this is a drop, a drop into the center of another fierce waterway. One will be pulled under, and dragged through the heart of the water—to the bottom, held there until oxygen has escaped and been given to the sea...this is where the body loses—is dragged to the edge, to the still water, the lifeless water...the edge is where the collector of the lifeless resides. One becomes the swallowed, where one must swallow the entity that has taken its soul—to be replaced with the water.

3.1

Along the Stony River's Gleam
Fingers Pressed Against the Glass
Next to the Prints Left
The Time Around There
And the Time Around Here
An Impenetrable Glare
To the Orphic Hymn
Crossing Light Bending
To the Shadowy Side
Though the Fog-Breath Builds
A Film Against the Surface
The Residue Slips Away
With a Return to Light
To Walk Against the Glass
And Let the Fingers Glide
Along the Curveless Glimmer
And See the Faceless Figure
An Image Made of Night-Mud
Where Voices Stop to Hear
Without Translucent Tones

7.1.3

smoothness
terrain
(solitude)
(miniaturism)
blindness from visibility

blindness from smallness
blindness from commonality
blindness from concealment
blindness from vastness
blindness from being material
sands (desert)
shifting (altered space)
un-conquerable
complete blindness—the changing arena
locating oneself at the point of the pivot—the center
circulation (thought)
nothing is completed
nothing needs completion
to complete a thought is to die in the desert
one must allow thought to always continue
there is no need for answers.
the desert is the land of covered remains—
to find the answer is to be buried by the sand.

glass—smoothness
jagged—broken—cracked
unknowable ground
too much visibility
traces—scratches and smudges
stains
watermarks
shatters and cracks lend as pathways
to see the end but not be able to reach it—to see everything
nothing can be concealed—nothing can be seen—
distorted view
to become luminescent
mirror image—the reflection—magnified
unknown distance
Moisture—slip
coldness—mist—fog
heat—humidity—steam

mountain—
altitude (summit)
pits (valley)
foreign land
trespassing
sightlessness (obstacles)
levels/blockages
repetition

multiplicity
traces
(footprints)
nightfall
(panic)
silence/quietness
the unbearably loud
the Torturous silence
amplified noises
(phantom noises)

creation of the monster
to become invisible
unseen from above or below
to go unseen by god and the devil
the unguided—desperate for either's stalking eye.
amongst the trees, hidden, covered within the layers
to lose sight—lose references
everything forms into the similar—foreign.
to seek rest where the ground is unable to be seen
blindness from obstacles becomes blindness from darkness
nothing sheds light—shadows are hidden
within the darkness...
unable to do their jobs, they sit and watch.
water is the only trail to follow
but to follow the water is to wake the animal during rest.
to see the way out...attempt to follow
and become lost all over again
to shrink as the mountain becomes small
to stay shrunken when the mountain grows...
to become the moss...
to be absorbed by the dirt...
lose skin to the rocks.
finding the trace of the human, following
the trail they carved
the others' footprints end.

3.2

Yet the mouth calls forth interminably, drawing you in until evasion is no longer possible. The mouth stands before you at the moment you realize there is no other way. Calling forth, pulling you in, all-consuming. Is it truth that this mouth demands? All one must do is stick the hand into a lock. But the stakes are higher in this game; you have more than just your hand to lose.

Skilled lock-pickers can wield stock tools with mastery and precision, but these instruments are always foreign to them. Instead, they craft their tools. Steak knives with scales removed, plied and heat-treated, balanced individually, to produce torque wrenches and picks. Each piece individually crafted for a single user, fitted uniformly for greater sensitivity. The pick becomes more than an appendage, more than an extension. In this way, the lock-picker tempts the validity of truth by sticking the hand in the mouth.

2.2

Out of carefully-strung notes and silences is the threat of a burgeoning discord.

A building never rises alone; simultaneously another structure is manufactured. Every live design contains a crooked skeletal formation intended for its creator. It illuminates the architecture with the heat and pain of one connecting a delicate framework that supports no passengers, with a promise of meticulous devotion.

These bones reflect light that emanates from the hands and teeth, and is absorbed within the hidden spine.

The reliable pieces of information, collected and hardened into the patterns and formulae that scaffold dreams, emerge as a gallows. Body is consigned to the becoming of this gallows, this tree. Tree, perch—not a death machine, though death is more than probable, but a place from which to catch suspensions.

1.2

Bodies with no shape: an illusion, a vision, a spectacle.

6.2

These bones are green.

Mold...moss...or simply, white has been overtaken. Perhaps white is overwhite, blinding white, white-hot; the first impurity, lost virginity, more a sin than an atonement; the lie is white (by way of truth's blackness), yet always stained, yellowed. The white of bone could be yellowed, but these eyes see them as green. Bone: singular substance (wait, look closer) exposed. Its greenness teems with growth, vile growth, imposed on a space that has been separated from growth. See them as green or not at all—otherwise you are staring at horizons, effigies. You believe that bone is white only because they made you cower at the overwhite—lacerate yourself a thousand times, sharpen the blade against osseous matter (my edge is for use if needed, though rust is beginning to accumulate)—see just how white bone is.

Bone, space for growth; bone, teeming with green.

Green bones, fallen in place. The fossil keeps asking for a name—no one answers. An interrogator, seducing as it accuses; rather, accusing with seduction. Reminders, remnants, calibrated bone—filed by the teeth of its burying—the time of things unknowingly cut by the betrayal of exposure.

They once said (forgive me if I misspeak) that the fossil gives history-as-stone, unbreakable; perhaps this is no longer the case, perhaps not yet the case. Now, though, the stone has been purchased broken. It demands a penalty for lost form—incompleteness. The fossil: stone-becoming-bone once again—the ancient cutting into the now, the then, the never. The fossil: accusing you, mocking you for your silence, silence laughs along and mocks you anew, your stupid gaze, you against stone. The fossil: demanding of a project— to invent names, to cut into time, to glue together gaps (only for a fresh tear), to hold bastard excavators accountable, to turn stone back into bone back into flesh—forbidden alchemy.

The age of penalties has fallen.

Razed lands, erosion, flooded with heat, ice, shards of parchment— the fossils of thought begging to be uncovered only to interrogate once more. A penalty paid once (one will be paid again—and then again), blood-letting, perishing. The fossil invites you in, leads you (stone in hand) to the banquet—a project of excavation that takes hold of you and will not loosen grip. Thought's death brought you back to this gallery of reckoning (all that has been fashioned by your hands stands ready to accost), this barren earth. Bend down, look closer (look closer)—vibrant flame of thought turned green stone.

You die there, in supplication, silent to your interrogator, filling in the gaps of the incomplete, wondering how the eyes of thought would see you if it were still alive.

You die there because you are mistaken. The flame never burned, there never was a complete, eyes plucked out before they saw you.

You die there because your hands are clumsy, you are overtaken, a world (shattered) upon another world (decayed) upon another world (torn) upon another (expelled), thought's fossilization will not let you out—bone-chippings, glittering in the darkness of your gaze.

A recourse: growth, in the hands of the accidental alchemist (hands sharpened as they are cut, bred for survival)—growth will be stone turned bone turned flesh.

Encased in that mongrel flesh, the accidental alchemist will dance on the bones of those who have fallen

                                drive them into the sediment of nothing

a new fossilization

1.3

Exhumation: to disinter actions, they must be intelligible; none are here. There is a quiet that remains and refuses to explain. The body is numb. Its nerve-endings resonate sound that evaporates, causing the frame to subdue in the wake of the split, deeper than any tearing.

5.3

The interior must be lacerated. This imperative demands that pain be deepened, not evaded. Instincts are informed by a long history of cowardice that stagnates rather than impelling toward a becoming. In order for there to be a dislodging, a jarring-loose, from this stagnation, a process of ever-deepening agony must be undergone; those things that the real does not permit are necessarily painful to obtain.

There can be no way out of this agony if it is to be deepened. This is why to have any potential this anguish must be stolen. A thing assaulted can always excuse itself from distress because it has not asked for it. Those who have withstood torture, and are ruined by it, have at their hands plenty of rhetoric, ideological ointments, and antibiotics to heal their wounds. This world produces the things that possess the potential to end it, but it also has an abundance of pacification for those who come into contact with agony: torture is an injustice; this regime is corrupt; as a being who has been tortured, I am ruined and possessed of no further potential; the cause for which I fought is not worthwhile. These are medicines to counter a vital illness, and none leads any further. These all allow for the conviction that violences are somehow mitigated by these narratives.

Stolen agony does not allow for such narratives to arise. This is not to say that a being who has agony inflicted upon it is undeserving. No body is exempt from this infliction. Those of unsought agony can justify the return to a comfortable, familiar reality; given the tightness of the grip with which this reality grasps—and all of the devices it prepares to heal the injured—all that is necessary to resurrect is a single excuse made. A world that relies on depriving feeling of anything at all; the thief who steals in order to feel something, even if it is painful; this leads to forfeiture of the right to excuse oneself, leaving only one trajectory to trace: a deepening.

The real is not simply some exterior force that acts upon the sovereign body; it has infiltrated the body, as well as the psyche, so that now in order to extricate it, one must slip the blade into safe territories. The body is exalted as something sacred, held close to oneself, as the inviolable vessel of one's being. Science attempts to locate all of the self somewhere in the body, thus creating the belief that it is what one must guard most closely. No. The body must become something upon which one inflicts, something to manipulate, and reform, something mutilated, in order that a transfiguration be made possible.

Inhabit dangerous, harmful spaces. To incise is not sufficient. One must do so repeatedly, constantly reopening scars, allowing them to heal just long enough so that the pain is felt anew with each incision. Keeping wounds open makes one infectious. By keeping the wounds on one's own body and consciousness open the chances that this disease will spread are increased. But it cannot be left to chance. Wounds must be opened on others as well. To automatically, mercilessly, and unwittingly corrupt everything with which one comes into contact. This is the sign of yawning and discomfort.

Do not underestimate the depths at which these roots run. To strike, claim victory, and move on to the next target will yield nothing. You are completely immersed in the real, and you are terribly outnumbered here. There are no allies, only definite and potential enemies that seek to heal the wounds cast upon yourself; these duties are performed masterfully. Only by constantly revisiting old harms can one anticipate an exit. It is not as if one declares dissociation from the real and is allowed a smooth severance. The real is constantly repairing itself, and in order to do so it repairs the bodies of its hosts, so it is essential never to cease illicit carvings. This is to make of oneself an instrument that no longer differentiates between the innocent and those who deserve what is about to happen. Everything is subject to this laceration. This being of indiscriminate infliction is the image of one who is perpetually foreign to its surroundings. In its presence, one senses that he is not dealing with someone like himself. Though this being of infliction understands the pain and destruction it causes, and could even comprehend the pleas it would hear from those it touches, it operates by a logic beyond them, one that will remain elusive to all who refuse to apply blades despite every natural impulse.

6.4

Ecstatic horror: for each thread, another labyrinth. I approach the machine trembling, sick, expelling fascination, expelling frenzied calm: the need, the compulsion to switch it on. I switch it on. Thread spun, metal hot to the touch (and to think, I cannot feel it)—for each thread, another labyrinth.

I answer to a machine.

Heaving under absent weight of labyrinth in the free fall of an atmosphere that asphyxiates. Threads, more labyrinths, labyrinth within labyrinth, upon labyrinth; the machine will not switch off. For each thread another labyrinth that (if followed) will lead into another.

Frailty: inability to stop weaving this misborn thread.

Fines paid for actions determined:
a cost for chance-stumbling-upon
the severed operation of such a frail apparatus.
So frail that it cannot switch off.

Thread, absent of color—as strange as it is familiar...rather, strange how familiar it is to weave around the palm; too many textures, absent of any. In these absences there is no panacea for our malformed condition, only the proliferation of more. Two paths (others to follow): either no longer see the absence, or nail it to flesh (engulf it with the machine's heat...to see absence burn). In the first, in loss, one fails to achieve a base realization: I am thread spun out of a machine that did not want to switch on, that does not know how to switch off.

Misborn thread.

Cords, fibrils, a pile on the ground, woven into a garment, for I am cold and that coldness will never leave me. I am a garment enveloped around another—weak coldness that lingers. Stretched, splayed. What to do but weave you around me? I am cold, I weave you around me.

To the second path: each thread is an interpretation;
yet, as cloth, each can burn.

Burn them as they fall to the ground;

there will be others to follow.

How does one light the ineffable aflame and not beg for more? No, precisely; beg for more. I drown in that thread, ruin my hands weaving a thousand garments, generating this heat that envelops. Heat generated by machine, consuming machine. Thread exhausting machine, impelling the price of its production, inflicting it back. I did not want to switch it on—skill hidden as that which is maladroit, the machinist as neophyte—but if not me, then one who swallows machine.

I heat up, I implode.

Compulsion is talent fitted to that of a machinist: the aimless spinning of my perception's thread (look back, look ahead, see how this has been spun).

I heat up, I implode.

I burn, this thread burns, the machine spins its last offering.

Remaining is that very absence, burning.

2.4

When the delicate, rarified air of the inner cavity is suddenly released into the atmosphere, the view is galvanizing. In the blank eyes of shaking meat, hypostasis is removed. To see and understand the victim as being overtaken and swallowed by something outside the mind, by something as close as the dysfunctional body. Frantic upheaval is no longer hidden within cerebral walls but quakes form tip to tip. It is more than love of spectacle that draws attention to such a painfully animated figure.

Fastened by the interruption, the dread of the emergence builds within the spectator until both sky and ground are pierced, until the whole of the world has been grasped by a span. There are a variety of seizures that can be experienced, and certain species have a voracious appetite. So much so that even when the spell lifts and the person returns seemingly not more broken than before, in the face of what should be reassuring, sleep becomes difficult.

These electro-physiologic phenomena manifest themselves as a mixture of disorientation, experiences of déjà vu, and overwhelming emotions. One wanders in a stupor while undergoing; victims are as unaware as passersby on the street. Consciousness sits to the side. In coming back, knowing that seizure has occurred is only understood by the familiar sense of memory loss and confusion.

This fluke cannot be allotted to the brain.

It sprouts from unmarked territories that are left open to affliction, and even hope to be susceptible...

...all the skill and natural talent constricts into a will to be dominated, to become a vessel. This sacrifice yields only blankness; there is no understanding of what occurs in a state of epiphania or possession. But the word is said and feeds into an awakening to something, somehow rearranged.

1.5

Hidden from the colors of the day, absorbed by the colors of the night, unleveling playgrounds emerge.

Body integrates into territory; it becomes its landscape. The body awakens, finding the skin impalpable: the skin of another surface. Here the verb 'to play' is enacted; infusion of enactment and creativity, a predilection and obversion.

Searchings for multiple points, interstices, and through these grows an awareness of invisibility; to disappear in the open space of everything. These spaces, playground and body, are where it becomes possible to find spores of the imperceptible, proliferating fungi.

6.5

As written: we will no longer bury our dead.

For this line, for this breezeless supposition, another one falls to the ground.

On the nude expanse, heels abrading the remains of nameless forms—fallen at the hands of finely-attuned audacity—one only finds the utter erasure of accountability in holding oneself accountable for stench that tarries.

The old operation, soon to pass: hands washed of blood, washed until they are chapped, skin chafed, as if the name and the epitaph would erase the consequences of this ceremony, this bedlam. No more names, no more epitaphs, the old graves will be not as much forgotten as they will be smothered. For each stratum of thought that has been erected, the expanse of unburied forms will outweigh them all in the sheer velocity of such an undertaking—line upon line, body upon body, even in restraint another falls, bearing down on the glass façade of existence, shattering, bending every trace.

Dictation (of a notion): the names alluded to here—names that have been spoken to a breaking-point, bodies buried then resurrected then buried again, endless cycle carried out in monolithic structures of pure indifference—must be forgotten. Finely-attuned audacity: they have passed, they will not be buried. Out of honor, out of love, they will not be buried.

Their writing is stench, this more a stench

for anyone who passes by
for the strata below
they will be made to inhale
to the point of their unburying.

5.6

The Mark: an involuntary carrier of a destiny

To bear a mark invisible to oneself, that is nonetheless apparent to
the *right* ones.

To be permanently scarred by contact with another.

To involuntarily, automatically infect/communicate by this mark.

The one who bears the mark cannot help
but to contaminate everything that is touched.

7.6

accessory—adornment—
the ornaments that become the body
missing—markings—history—scars (nudeness) (tan lines)
appurtenance—paraphernalia—the supplement

Mirror: to see it, to see it before it escapes the compact, it thought it
had more time, time to linger, time to watch, to see it escape, to see
the recognition, the reflection that was always there, and always left
on time (early), to catch the glimpse, to trick the watcher...when
found: it must reassign the finale, rework the visual of the body,
rewrite the obituary.

2.6

A tetanus seeps into the writhing space of the cavity in order to
build a base of operations, to activate and convert this rudimentary
opening into a susceptible and vibrant apparatus that breathes, that
deals in electric caresses and damages.

5.7

The terror of something expertly-crafted, merciless,
and automatic...the terror in the realization that there are
subjects—who are not likely to be easily detectable—
who design and build these apparatuses

Cold in its metallic smoothness

Hot in its movement

Circular motion turned linear

To be lost in its complexity, to be seduced by its elegance...
to fall victim to its processes

To be in the presence of something that is not understandable, that
will not differentiate
between one piece of matter and another,
whether they be made of fabric or flesh

3.7

Stepping into the noise, armed with refined sensitivity, periphery
vanishes by the pull into the mouth. Periphery becomes the center,
centrality extends across everything. The engagement begins once
the lock projects its interiority into the lock-picker; in turn, the lock-
picker allows exteriority to vanish. One sees but cannot be seen,
touches but cannot be touched. It would be a mistake to say that, in
this state, they recess into themselves. In fact, the opposite is true. So
far from being encapsulated within their own interiority—an
intensity far from the captivity of passion—this is a moment of
consignment, one marked by gravity, sensuality, and rhythmic
breathing. This is the secret of the lock-picker, allowing the origin of
the question of escape to become obsolete. This secret is best kept
because it is one that cannot be spoken.

Without a reason to engage, the lock-picker searches and seeks out
barriers. Yet without an obstacle to surpass, the only recourse is
evaporation. The molecules are taken up into the wind and spread
into spaces that cross between light and darkness. Migratory, they
seek out impasses to pass through for the sake of continuous
transmission. The difference between the thief and the lock-picker
is that the first has a goal, a prize. The other simply seeks movement.
Migratory, and incapable of exile, distasteful of open spaces, they

follow the walls, specifically to find the breaches.

In what ways does a rock generate sensitivity? Rocks are quiet, sometimes too quiet, but we hear their rapturous whispers when they form a crowd. When the roars of passion abrade the palate, combining and colliding, breaking off and against skin, their surface zones of layered speckles extend themselves to minor vibrations. The slightest movement— when the torsion wrench is used to first test the give of the cylinder—reveals itself not in the fingers, but in the toes. This is to say the vibration that extends itself from the cylinder moves through and across the body to the most grounded point. A dance, all too corruptible, bare but not exposed. The first movements are always the most awkward; how to give and how to receive. After the first movements there follows a sigh, a release, to begin a new rhythm that need not be bound to what came before; at the same time, a final recognition to the beating that will soon disappear. This marks a passage, just as when blood shoots through a valve in the veins; in the same sense, the constriction of the valve pushes forth, propels.

The give of the cylinder indicates an admittance whereby the precession to follow is already granted forgiveness. A cylinder that does not give...but this is a gesture that cannot simply be taken.

2.7

A cannibal word or image allows us to stray and return, to disassemble and absorb—speaking things which neither you nor the familiar would even know how to begin to pronounce.

133

5.8

To have reached the limit of what can be absorbed; how to take a world that absorbs everything and drown it in its own toxic substances?

At present the world finds itself populated mostly by entities that prolong its life. Yet violent individuals continually arise, as if these arrivals were accidental, anomalous, interruptions of the process. These violent potentialities arise as the products of a world that is attempting a suicide. Without exception, this thing produces beings of a catastrophic species.

Look around: the world that surrounds is already in ruin.

This thing has reached its saturation point; it can absorb no more of the filth that it has produced. It is maintained by the efforts of its carriers that now rely upon it. The final turn is to similarly drown the entities that selfishly nurse this dying world. Unceasingly, at all given and stolen opportunities, toxic substances seep in through the crumbling façade.

1.8

Its tones intoxicate the numb anatomy of the dormant as one enters a labyrinth in the making; too many rooms to find a way back. The undertones of regional belonging intensify the lullaby, furthering the unexpected jaunt; no one can avoid from listening to the nonsensical chorus of enticement.

Its inaudible fragments of sound captivate the eardrum, one expression blankets the silence: a shattering. It originates where the perceived becomes strange and stranger. The shards cut through walls of space to distort its capabilities. One needs nothing but the ear to ingest an excess of potential beginnings. This calling resonates with the body; those who want to be lost should listen. In these rooms, stolen treasures are found; copies of one's "misplaced" trinkets brought here without memory. They are unrecognizable, and molder in the absence. The emptiness of these rooms waits for no one.

4.8

The town: streets devoid of movement

rustling, dead leaves dragged against pavement, breeze, awakened
branches, dry, leafless

at the foot...the clock tower...rusting toll, the bell reverberates,
winding trees encircling, deserted, decrepit, halted hands, at the
twelfth hour, long ceased to move

at the foot...the small town...against the wall, ruins...
faint cracks: breaks of footsteps, traversing across paths unmarked

at the foot...the fallen wall...small openings, light,
in-between, the conflagration of trees, branches,
bony branches, and leaves

a mist takes shape...formless beings unearth, within the sea of dead
leaves—a passing figure, a sifting, black mass...

There are others

rambling amidst the stillness of this town (sounds: non-silence),
heaviness, a pressing tone, the lowest key of an organ

Inaudible. Monumental. Proportion.

The Rains...unsuspected...

the windows of houses, visible patches of carved stone, cut-off
doorways, sharpened rooftop angles, inter-woven pathways, braiding
along the open spaces flaming orbs...
floating funereal lamp posts, damp wooden benches, vacant...all
entangled within the mass, withered trees and desiccated branches

slow shifts that slip to dark, spaces well defined, borders surrounding
forest, desertion ingrains

inexhaustible...fireless...smokeless...burning...
devouring flames, fumes rise, seep, linger over landscapes

This town, an island. Surrounded.
This town, consumed. Absent

aerial views, high altitude, entirety, distance, clarity...

Nothing escapes.

inaudible, pressing tones

Night has slipped.

7.9

The Rat

Residue
Leftovers
Oil (secretion)
Saliva
Coat (covers the fur)
Separation (water)
Slips (after the subject does not exist)
Remains (what remains indicates its presence)
Sediment (extracting the fats)
Impressions (language)
Imprints (representations)
Mood (lingering)
Event (the aftermath)
Gathering (bodily and environmental
collective produces the oils)
Gift (the piece that is left over after the rest has been used)
Rarity
Peculiarity
Curiosity

What remains is what indicates its presence.

There is safety in the wall, entrance can be found within
the cracks, the innumerable crevices, where there is something
splintered, but nothing protrudes, where there is no light to catch
the wooded, abbreviated doorway...
the one without a visible opening.

To follow this line—across its ledge—across its shadow—
and access the terminal.

Alliances can be found within this calcified space,
where there are others—they will allow you to reside,
but on the outside, the others cannot protect.
For, once exiting these dust-laden hallways, there lives
the giant who shakes ground, angers, but also jumps
at the sight (and runs). In this stadium, there is no retaliation, only
spaces that grey and leave oily residue on
the one who rubs against them. Remember this location
(the trace it leaves)— for, if returned, necks break...
poisons are consumed, and ground becomes glue...

If positioned in this, have no expectation of the others—
no one is loyal outside of the wall.

1.10

The limit erases and therefore creates the non-existent. There is no touch in touching if touching is limited to sound. There is no sight in seeing if seeing is limited to hearing...

    (circular) (disorienting) (without origin) (lost) (in too deep)
    (implicated) (undifferentiated) (camouflaged/blended)
    (co-opted) (repetitive) (duplicated) (mirage)

7.10

There is a surface that it will encounter,
created to enable its fall.
In this space it will believe strength and balance—
elude the void within the ring, learn that surface exists only in
pattern, upon the end of its journey...
it begins again. This is a creation of holes,
a gaping space where one is meant to slip.

2.10

Drawn to the dark slits of their mouths, strange air collects to fill membranous shells. Separated so completely from any musculature, ligature, or bone, animation appears to have been stopped, only for a moment. Integument left loose—hollow and thin, even so perfectly lifted—gains its own face.

Beneath the surface, shiftless air forms locked expressions. There can be no meeting of the gaze, and no understanding why. The head becomes the point of absentia, its face the dreamless dead-end in which all focus descends beneath the lower eyelid, where all tiredness gathers in a knot.

These skins that portray elegant states of the devitalized, living masks which no one can wear or inhabit. Aged skin conveying ageless creatures whose slightly shifting appearances thread for us a deep-sea experience. The elongation of delicate moments stretches their necks, craniums, and mouths, becoming too fragile to live. Darkness and stillness bury the witness; no movement is allowed except in an inescapable sleep. Nothing can be accounted for. Nothing can be seen. To be left as if one has soaked in water for days. Feeling that this unnatural place, that is contrary to you, that has vaccuated you, has become a home.

2.11

The night is a time for demon-building. Images of space allow one to feel heavy and vast, naked and suspended, clouded and terribly clear...

Against the black, each cosmic thing—planet, asteroid, star, etc.— emerges as its own complete object, perfect...alien unto itself...belonging and not belonging to the surrounding depths. The strangeness proceeds because there are demons at work.

Each presence emits a halo that softly melds into the fabric of a suspicious canvas. Particles that could never meet are so entwined that they are made to be inextricable. What transpires in the body of the shadow and of the night is an absconding darkness. It disseminates ever further in order to persevere...and in its departure, in its absence, remains the irrefutable draw of its fibers.

There is no owning, no belonging to the night. It exists as night in order to escape, to be out of reach but close enough to make us tremble, to surround and penetrate but have nothing to say.

The night is never a mantle.

First there was darkness and then there was light. The night does not want you. It does not share that kind of hunger. If there is any seduction, it is perpetrated by you.

Mirror without a surface, the merging with yourself loses all masturbatory connotation and a new intimacy is born. A new indecency. Deep shadows bring with them moments, passings too powerful, too unraveling to remain transient. These corners, these edges in space wound and fill every opening. Every future step is ghosted by a shadowing of quiver.

If one could only contain the presence of the night, if one could leave the region unmapped with ominous signs of danger, "here be monsters" slashed in red...but the region leaks, and there are times during the day when the darkest night emerges, and you are left to your own resources, to producing your own active forces; hardening the body of an object, singling out a stone before it is stone and sending it out into the night. Incising new meridians.

1.11

When the room is entered, everything is gone.
Once inside nothing will be the same. There are stages and steps, and those who enter do not remember them. Everything is embraced first, and then nothing is left.

4.11

they too will answer to the whips and blows of their brothers

he gathers among the images, a tiny sparkle in our guilt

Alluvial Dictums

...your animal instinct shows itself in ways that cannot be fathomed,
even by you

...the breath of your breath's gasp betrays the voice of the exiled

...the heat of exhaustion is the terror at their gates

...the peacock's feather

...tasks are buried beneath the rancor of a broken coil

...agitation reveals the vile stillness of a stone's shadow

...the quickened glances

...innocence is the revulsion of a stillborn fecundity

...a fugitive secret can release you if only you would allow it

... the beckoning, like a voice a step beyond the prow

...the unspoken world sifting behind the curtain of every day

...to break the already-shattered glass of a world in ruin

Alluvial Dictums

...*there is no sign of green—I cannot bear the howling*

...*it is rather shallow now*

...*the image imprinted inside, he began the playback, not of the event,
but of the impact it caused*

...*the colors are all gone, along with the sounds*

...*I am biting again*

...*the others are no longer heard in the background*

...*all days spent within the hollows of a watchword*

...*a whiteness that burns*

...*what is owed to the invisibles*

...*a room of words, a room of gestures, a lapse between doorways*

...*across the room, a faint scar is visible, towards which the dismembered
gravitate*

...*the defective machine wants to survive*

1.12

Mosaics painted only in black, washed with the agitation of music, the agitation that creates all music, revealing a keyhole without a lock. The key, a rotting piece of brass from the furthest house on the left, from the block lined with maple trees, caged animals, and square mailboxes. Colors of the mosaics burn through, the street becomes clearer; the brass pauses; the trees sway in this direction; the mailboxes are still; the trees sway in that direction; the animals rattle in anticipation. The lights are off, the lights are always off.

3.12

Observe the surrounding environment...search for the crevices that are always there. These are not just weaknesses in the structure. They are the medium-zones in which impossibility begins to become possible. Without these miniscule arenas of maneuverability, everything would be fixed. Perfection would become too real, and death too visible. A structure without space is too perfect because it allows for nothing; not the passage of air, water, and not even words or abstractions. The exit strategy is always ready-built into the framework (monitor what is overlooked...seek out the path of least resistance). The lock will come when it is called; it is important not to call on it before it becomes necessary. The lock is always there, but it cannot be recognized too soon. We believe that we call forth the lock, though in fact, the lock calls on us. The tiny space, the mouth that never closes, from which an interminable vibration evokes a lustful sense of purpose. But what can be done indirectly will always serve us better than that which entices a direct route. If this requires climbing a tree to the second story to shimmy a window open, then so be it. The skilled lock-picker will try to escape from an unnecessary encounter. In a game where winning is just prolonging the inevitable and losing is the only recourse for life, the lock-picker makes the aim to suspend the game.

7.12

This is a place where one finds itself multiplied—
by nature, the fold's duality ensures that it will lose its way—
get lost in the structure—
(finds itself on the lowest level,
the bottom stair).

It will see itself hidden in corners,
disguised in the cracks and waiting in the blind spots.

It seeks the weakened lines, and follows the wrinkles...
but this is not the map for escape...these are the traces,
the footprints of the others...the ones who already attempted
leaving but instead were buried further in the levels.

This is the space where one will always find
itself deeper in the divides.

6.13

Building of force: turn word into gesture.

A secret, half-birthed—the portion revealed calls for an end to all that has been seen (what, then, does the portion obscured crave?). The body cries out for this unveiling—words, utterances, echoing in the inner chambers of the ear because they are only echoes, no original to be found. They consider this point given and concede nothing—except the need remains for a driving-out, a regurgitation; language is dead yet we cannot cease to speak. The body asks: can gestures buy the right to end this frenzied circulation?

Building of force: turn word into gesture…becoming the very thing tracking you down…word becomes silence becomes gesture.

Now writing is abandoned. The cold machinery of this exploitation exists to generate apocryphal signs, to project fractured war-performances. The hand moves, no longer to scratch dissipating thoughts that can be easily scattered, but to gesture, to spawn phantom limbs that will not leave you, becoming mist intertwined with flesh. The gesture seals gaps in its motion as it creates others, evades enveloping rabble, continues to circulate past the edge of the word, past the border of the page.

Gestures, interminable: reverberations that project themselves
within a loop that scatters.

Gestures, contradictory (necessarily so):
betrayal, unknown intent, unknown effect.

Gestures, contaminating: a viral pulse, an echo that pollutes.

Gestures, beyond the word, beyond human:
sacrificing the body from which they originate
in order to breed illegitimate desires.

Gestures, beyond expression,
assemblage of a new mechanism:
rabid hearts beating with ice,
hands of stone trimmed, cryptic missive carved.

Gestures, both cost and gift.

Gestures, operation of the war-performance.

3.13

When the hands are rubbed together a cauldron erupts, emitting boiling water and steam to commingle with the stale and tepid air. Liquefied molten rock floods into the alluvial strains, which guide into the surrounding ocean, and tempers the backflow, allowing for an unremitting release. Beneath all this activity there lies a plane of receptiveness not limited to material viability. Remember this: when the hands rub together the world shakes a little. This act allows one to feel across another object; it allows for the infinite space of the in-between to carry the sounds of a prisoner's laughter.

Everything beyond this point is an enactment: auditioned, practiced, staged, and performed. The staging is important for the purpose of unleashing. Unleash the listening—unleash the feeling—unleash the seeing; when this becomes possible, then certainty can finally rest its head. The hook pick slips into the mouth, an intercession, the tool of choice. The hook pick—like a single curved finger, also called the feeler. This is the most commonly used pick, but it is the most difficult to master. It requires a steady hand, a balanced body, and a regulated rhythm of heart and lungs; otherwise, the vibrations find a way to escape. The intercession begins to bleed out, an effusion of signs, one manipulating the other, yet there is nothing to see here. The feeler counts the pins, feels for the ones with the most give, and for the ones that need to be soothed into position. One single swoop of the feeler is all that should be necessary to determine how to proceed. The torsion wrench and the pick work together, one tightens its grip but only with a faint amount of pressure, only what is necessary; the other lifts the pins one-by-one until they catch. One twists, the other lifts; one constricts, the other plays; in order to operate within this space one must become mechanical; a mechanical reflection of the mechanism.

1.13

The wrong happening—
mistake (blindness) (blending)
warping (boats against wind)

5.14

> To be infinitely suggestible—
> this is permanent and perfected innocence
> no ideology or impetus of one's own
>
> To move as the world affects one
>
> To be immediately distracted by the negation
> of any potential proposition,
> and for anything imaginable to be possible
>
> To have lost the desire to form beliefs
>
> To bear an openness without limit, and to be paralyzed by the
> infinite possibilities
>
> To be made the enemy of morality and judgment
>
> To be unworldly—this thing operates by a foreign logic

3.14

The skilled lock-picker stops just before the moment that it becomes necessary to peer into the crooked incision. Vision is no longer necessary. Part of the training is to learn when to leave behind the things that blind the senses. To blind yourself in order to avoid blindness. A practice that cannot be taught, only learned.

1.14

No longer a part of anything, nothing takes over the room. A body enters, and under the guise of everything, it waits.

4.14

space ingests space
        depth
images sprout from the recesses...
stretched hallways
abandoned
        dark
infinite rooms
        yesterday's color
dampened stairwells

splintered handrails
fissured ceilings of exposed, rusted pipes...

This place: damp
This place: dirty

   the leper's vault:
      spilling sweet remnants of excess
        ...aimless...

This place: old
This place: past

a flicker...a flash...
as old and forgotten as the second
       ....turning a corner...

This place: condemned
This place: dying

always on the brink of ruination
   the image of an image finds itself...
      decaying

   ...it stands...
      hardened through time

This place: residual
This place: unmoved
This place: fortified

autumnal wind bends through the enclosing fence
a lock rests on the gate
...others have been here before...

walls, written on
   marks live on the crumbling surface

windows, broken
doors, open

no wish to enter the chasm of this aberrant city...
   evidence of recent life is now lost
      place behind time's fading veil...
no signs of life within the metallic bowels

This place: past-life
This place: dressed in flight
This place: perfumed presence

odor…drifting scent,
living inside these walls…
another

Pass through open doors,
a punctured cavity…imploded

watched,
trespassed
                victims, molding
in every room,
further into the depth of this structure

everything remains here
there is nothing here

burning, slips the dark
the rancid hand summons the depths

flavor—
grittiness strangles tongue

everything—
quiet
            minimal sounds
            imperceptible shifts
    nerve-sting
            droplets
    leaves now charred
    wind-cries

                rooted mud

breath—gripped
what was here…what has gone…
        Escaped

faceless entity
without limbs
            without form

...fills grief

misplaced:
      a loss
words

This place: a liquid curtain
          ashamed
          unworthy
          grasping presence

without entering
        the midst
staircase
 deep basements
 subterranean levels
 wrought-iron frames
 pillars
 suspended ramps
      steel wire
 immeasurable foundations

lingering, wandering,
searching for its own reflection
it seeks to know itself
projected
      a larger space
fragmented, lost
turning toward itself

...into another room...

Every room:
      a witness
        a sacrifice

It is the loss,
   the objects,
      that corners the structure

1.15

The doors were left open. The doors are always left open. The locks were designed uniformly, their keys branded on the body. Pieced together with inanimate objects, they moved through one another under arches, passageways, and through crevices to find leftover body parts in ordinate boxes; hands, eyes, toes, singular, defined. They played with them, lost them, only to find them again; they attempted to animate them but could not. And, though without life, the knocking on the door stiffens them.

6.15

Ephemeral flood, existence is unstrung.

Paralysis: this bolus, this undigested mass, burrows further with every breath. White light cracks the edge of the mouth, splinters one's field of vision with loose speed, damaging velocity; an incisionist, a surgeon of forms, taping one's eyelids open to the carnival gathered around.

I know these specters, I have seen them before.

They know me, they have seen me before.

The day after the last night. The day has come, no more sleep to be had. The day has come, sleep has ended, we are not awake. Paralyzed, a world unstrung; there are those awash in sempiternal inertia who cannot see it (the dreamer who refuses to rouse—enemy on the horizon, and the dreamer refuses to rouse), massive lump of contradictory force bearing down, dying in not knowing how to die.

Not-asleep, not-awake—reconfigured sight attuned to the carnival, the arcade of penumbras. Cracking the sternum, minimal time remains. When survival is on the line, one does not wish to speak— one only wishes to move.

Bolus, born of sleep—music, poetry, language (rambling, a stranger's voice), revelation, sound, pleasure, pain—you fell into it, your body contorted out of horror, you fell again. The moment before sleep arrived, you did not hear your own voice, you heard another's murmur (despite all this writing it has yet to be recalled).

Promises are threats. A particular history, a particular time, born of this threat—encased in a garbage contract, signed, endlessly signed, a culture of dreams that has produced nothing but signatures in faded ink-stains.

False sleep. The dream, stripped of evanescence, believed, loved, maintained, emptied of dark matter, void of voids, broken spell— someone flew too close to the bolus disguised as black sun.

Not-asleep, not-awake, the day after the last night has come.

The terror is there, head resting on stone, body being written upon. The terror does not emanate from within, it is in the fog of gathering: the one not-asleep/not-awake, the bolus, the specters gathered as a cloud of witnesses. No longer asleep to an awareness: as much as we are haunted by the fog, we also haunt. To be not-awake, yet aware of this haunting—the bolus threatens because it has been seen sitting there, bearing down, consuming what it can in death throes.

Not-asleep. Not-awake.

Calm terror. Awakening to never being awake. The risk of those who calm themselves in the irreality of paralysis: a playground, a carnival they wish to join, specters proliferated, calming terror of the not-asleep, not-awake. The greater risk of those (if only one could be found) in the day after the last night who accelerate the suffocation, endure it, who writhe the conjured body in hopes of a separation.

5.16

This is where stolen flesh is stockpiled. This place is no more proper a home for these bodies than is the real, and yet, uncontested, something has stolen them. Silently, unnoticed, bodies find themselves in this alternate space apart from what is real. Some have found an escape toward which they have been planning and working for a long time. Others find themselves seduced by an acute sensitivity for something that is imperceptible to others—and even they only perceive it as an eerie presence—that takes a hold of them and demands that nothing take precedence over it. What is meant to take place here, however, is unclear. Each one senses that something has come for him, specifically. They feel that it is taking hold of them and that they cannot attempt to harness it because they do not know what to turn it towards. There is a logic to it; it is not random, and yet that logic, though discernible, is elusive, foreign, and ultimately ominous. This project has come as a stranger, and without concern for who they are or what they seek to achieve as living subjects it has demanded their attention. To master, control, and wield this thing would require understanding, which is lacking above all else.

Still there are those of another species who are here without the advantage of being aware of their surroundings. This ignorance allows them to continue to operate in much the same way they would were they truly unbound from this fetid space, and this escapism allows for harms of the highest degree to be inflicted upon them without detection. To ignore this space of the stolen bodies is to turn one's back on a ceaseless force of consumption. Subjectivity is unstrung, lacking ideology and anything that can properly be called a "world." These beings occupy spaces, not worlds; they follow whims, imperatives even, but not ideologies; and they forfeit action for a sort of drifting. There can be no pleas or arguments here. Things simply happen.

Some of these bodies are the ones who were lured to travel. None of them travel out of discontentment with their prior residence. It is a curiosity, not the desperation of discontentment, that moves these entities, and among the locales to which they travel is the real world. They touch everything. Amidst the rotting oblivion of the real, among its anesthetized wanderers, are agents of further, accelerated decay. They travel here to claim more bodies and to increase the gravity acting on what is already in a state of decline. Those things that are not useful must be made to decay more rapidly, more completely, so as to open space for potential happenings, even those with catastrophic effects.

Here bodies are eviscerated. Lives (and all baggage associated with this word) evaporate, are rendered meaningless. These bodies become spaces of potentialities that supersede the lives that inhabited them before they were stolen away to this place.

The space of these stolen bodies moves alongside the real world, in fact, encompassing it. It is the void in which everything is immersed, and because of its vastness it is invisible. To attempt to step outside of it, to examine it—to verify its existence—is preposterous. Some sense an inescapable presence felt in the shoulders. The rest fall to it regardless of their insensitivity for its effects. There can only be movement within it, regardless of whether one's location within is acknowledged. There can be no transcendence or escape of this void, only a nod given to its permanence.

6.16

To turn one's back on a world is not a terminus—it is exposure to a host of other worlds. And as one turns away he finds that it is not he who turns, but the empty pressure of the host turning him: calling, beckoning, beleaguering.

In the wake of this mutter, one's irrelevancy is under siege.

The call: as gentle as it is brutal, inviting in its fraudulence, generous in its pillaging. The call offers as much resistance towards as it does comfort away; beckoning the drunken-lustful, beleaguering the already-exhausted only to hold them accountable for their thirst. Appearance upon appearance of comfort: you succumb in your comfort, you succumb even more turning vertiginously towards the call.

The call: a call to violence.

Turning, exposure, interrogation—none of these experiences are regarded as passive, as lullabies (scream and silence conflate here, the muffle, the gasp—the call comes as a lullaby of what scream and silence are asking for). Ecstasy as anesthetic, sublimity as stupor— you have been given these in your comfort. The call asks how much more can be endured, how much more can be sacrificed.

The shadowlands impose, an existence held at blade's edge.

One must traverse beyond endurance, enact bastard legacies: an alchemist willing to mix poison and nectar (blood and water)—one who betrays a world in order to betray the countless others that have called him.

Pacts of betrayal.

The call cries out for such a betrayal—lest there be a failure to live up to the tepid snarl of its bargaining.

The call: not a thought, not an art, not a philosophy, not an aesthetic—it calls one in mirroring itself in the absence of these. Stamped, scratched, marked on the skin: each instance of ignorance is a laceration, yet each gasp of affirmation bleeds one dry all the more. The call is there, draining, waiting to be drained.

A host of worlds await—
bastard legacies to be had, enduring alchemy.

Violence
propelled past the crest of its own fury; past the tender stroke of your cheek; past the sinking pit of idiocy that is its heart, its love; past the mass graves in its wake

past the summer afternoon
its breeze grazed
the flower in your assailant's hand
petals unfolded in anticipation

past history and time, already erased. This is what the call freely gives and takes—if anything, an opportunity to turn to the world one has abandoned, and bend it back to the table of negotiation.

1.16

A distraction that startles. More than an unexpected moment, it is a trap. The lion's mouth. Its fangs are not only locks, but windows and knives. The danger brings a calm, overcoming the nerves; the pulse weakens, the beating disappears. Silence surrounds what used to be panic; in this compound, fear becomes a waiting room where colors become their opposites.

It is a shipwrecker's dream, desolate and effacing in the ripples of scorching air; the malady of antecedents feverishly inhabits the body and draws its weapon...since there is little warning and no

156

traction, the only vestiges left are broken finger nails.

4.16

One is already on the way of grasping its faintness (toward what is most unlike itself).

2.16

The Power of Useless Objects

Moving Pictures: Curious Literatures
Hearing Voices, Hearing Sounds
Words Not to be Trusted: Discarded
Texts/Pseudologies/Conspiracies
Cast-off Toys
Method of Payment: Circulations of Worthlessness

Further Reaches into Obscurity

Entrance occurs without need, without desire

Stale air and uneventful silence amplify the palpitations of Useless Objects

Harmlessness disappears—peculiar things are never amusing

Having outlived lives, things gain weight in the palm of your hand

Nothing is found

Nothing is easily set back down

gnOme is a secret press

specializing in the publication

of anonymous,

pseudepigraphical, and apocryphal

works from the past, present, and future.

Anything than which a greater

or a lesser cannot be posited

cannot be named. – Nicholas of Cusa

gnOme is acephalic. Book sales

support the authors.

GNOMEBOOKS.WORDPRESS.COM

Other titles from gnOme

Made in the USA
Lexington, KY
02 June 2017